# DUNCIAD MINOR

# DUNCIAD
# MINOR

*An heroick poem*

*by*

A. D. HOPE

*Profusely annotated by A.A.P. and A.P.*

MELBOURNE UNIVERSITY PRESS

First published 1970
Printed in Australia by
Wilke and Company Limited, Clayton, Victoria 3168 for
Melbourne University Press, Carlton, Victoria 3053
Great Britain and Europe: ISBS Inc., London
USA and Canada: ISBS Inc., Zion, Illinois 60099
Registered in Australia for transmission by post as a book
Designed by Norman Quaintance

ISBN 0 522 83997 5
Dewey Decimal Classification Number A821.3

# PREFACE

The following poem is now something of a museum piece and my reasons for publishing it after a lapse of twenty years as well as my reasons for writing it in the first place require some explanation since it began partly as a private joke never meant for publication and partly as an exercise in a form of literary criticism with which most readers nowadays are not familiar.

In 1950 the Australian Broadcasting Commission got up a series of literary talks entitled: 'Standard Works I'd Like to Burn'. It was perhaps a rather silly title and not a very bright idea in any case, but reappraisal of established literary reputations was then very much in the air and it gave an opening which promised some lively controversy. A number of well-known literary critics were invited to take part, including myself and my old acquaintance A. A. Phillips. He was then senior English master at Wesley College, Melbourne, and known as one of the outstanding teachers of the subject in Victoria. I was senior lecturer at the University of Melbourne. The speakers were encouraged to be provocative and to hit hard, but to keep the tone of their attacks reasonably light and amused and, as I recollect, most of us managed to do this. I chose Matthew Arnold as my butt. Arnold is not difficult to make fun of but he was a great man for whom I have liking and respect and I am now rather ashamed of my performance which consisted mainly of scoring points rather than of serious criticism. Mr Phillips chose the works of Alexander Pope and though his tone was light and suggested a certain humorous exaggeration, it was a serious enough attack on Pope's standing as a poet. Indeed it took up the long-standing debate initiated by the romantic poets and given its most forceful expression by Matthew Arnold in a famous essay, *The Study of Poetry*. It pointed this traditional depreciation of Pope as a poet by comparing a passage from *An Essay on Man* unfavourably with Keats's 'Ode to a Nightingale'. Since I regard Pope as one of the very greatest of English poets, my blood very naturally began to boil as I heard Mr Phillips in the opening passages of his talk describe him in terms such as these:

an industrious enough craftsman, if not always a very good one, who chose to earn his living in one of the only ways open to an educated English Catholic in the early eighteenth century . . . a moderately skilful purveyor of spite and platitudes . . . our best purveyor of verbal reach-me-downs—and that is about all he is good for.

I sat down immediately the talk was over and wrote the following couplet and posted the second line to the speaker:

> Phillips, I heard you talk on Pope tonight;
> O that the *Dunciad* were again to write!

He replied at once: 'Hope, why not write it? I am sure you would not find the mediocre fleering at mediocrity beyond your powers'. By next morning my indignation had cooled and I was better able to make allowances for the tone of humorous exaggeration in which the talk had been couched. After all I was not in a much better position in view of the sarcasms I had levelled at Arnold. Nevertheless I felt that Mr Phillips should be paid in his own coin. I had long felt a desire to try my hand at the art of mock heroic; the reply to my couplet set me thinking of how Pope or Dryden might have taken up such a challenge; and I had a term off from university teaching. I began work and informed Mr Phillips that the poem was on the way and received a reply in heroic couplets which concluded:

> Since Imitation is your Art's full scope,
> Complete your humble mimicry of Pope,
> And when you come to pen a New Edition
> Select a target who deserves perdition,
> And, lest your Muse be labelled merely ribald,
> Assail a Cibber, not this honest Theobald.

This delighted me with the idea that the writer might be tempted to a reply in kind. In that case I might have invited him to join with me in publishing the two poems together. Unfortunately I did not then think to issue the challenge and he did not rise to it of his own accord, though recently he told me that he had sent me a further set of couplets and a letter which was mainly an appreciation of the poem. Unfortunately these never reached me, nor did I realize, as I might have, that Mr Phillips was just as unwilling to enter this contest in 'debunking' as I had been, and chose Pope for his attack mainly because he thought I had overpraised him in an earlier broadcast talk.

When the poem was finished, I had it typed and sent him a copy, having no intention of publishing what was intended as a private interchange and as an exercise, for my own satisfaction, in an older form of poetry. And there the matter has rested for twenty years. But by degrees copies got into circulation in typescript and I began to receive invitations from editors and publishers to make it public. I have always refused this, though I have allowed some excerpts of general satire on the state of modern literary criticism to appear in *Meanjin*, *Melbourne University Magazine*, and *Southerly*. If I have now changed my mind, it is because I am aware that once a work has achieved a certain amount of notoriety and copies are in circulation, it is impossible to suppress it and that eventually, even if after the author's death, it is likely to see publication. And this may occur at a time when there is no opportunity to explain the circumstances or to put the controversy in its proper setting. Not to publish in this way would seem to me to be unfair to Mr Phillips whom, apart from his attack on Pope, which I still reject, I have always regarded as a friend and whose standing as a critic I respect and admire. In particular, for the original to see print, in a world so full of bad and spurious critics, would seem poor justice and could only lead readers to conclude that I had intended a personal attack rather than a literary satire.

I have therefore revised the poem as it was in 1950, when it was primarily directed to answering the case against Pope and therefore mainly concerned with Mr Phillips as a critic of Pope. By adding two books of Funeral Games, I have turned the main attack against certain famous literary critics of our time, whose influence on literature and on the study of literature has, I believe, been pernicious, and against the superfoetation of literary criticism itself. The disagreement between myself and Mr Phillips stands on the firm basis of the older criticism. His is the romantic view, mine the classic or neoclassic. We are both old-fashioned enough to take this debate seriously. He believes I am wrong, and I believe he is wrong, on an issue which contemporary criticism tends to regard as unimportant. But though we may disagree on this issue, both of us, I believe, are in the position of critics who regard their function as that of serving literature, whereas much of the newer criticism parodied in the Funeral Games appears to me to view literature as something the critic exploits as his material and swamps in needless and gratuitous explication.

I should say a word about the nature of mock epic as a method of satire. It may appear to be holding *persons* up to ridicule and contempt when in fact it is aiming its laughter at theories and ideas. Because its mode is comic and its form narrative, it must present its critical points through persons and actions. Its method is to bring out intellectual or political and social issues by exaggeration and burlesque. In this it has much in common with the art of the political cartoonist who, in representing political figures in travesty, is concerned not with their actual appearance but with their political views. We all take this for granted because the cartoonist's is a living art. But mock epic is not, and is more apt to be misunderstood as a personal attack.

Because its method is travesty and exaggeration for comic effect, I have made no pretence of being strictly fair to the figures I have chosen as the butts of my ridicule. For many of them I have the greatest respect. Dr Leavis, outside his ill-considered attack on Milton and his over-estimate of D. H. Lawrence, has been one of the great seminal influences in contemporary criticism. The excesses of his followers cannot be blamed on him but on the natural tendency of disciples to carry things too far. But in a poem of this sort he properly appears as an eponymous figure standing for the whole

'Leavisite' school. The crass absurdities of the propounders of the so-called Intentional Fallacy cannot fairly be charged against the original scholarly and balanced article by Wimsatt and Beardsley, which gave rise to them. Nor is Wilson Knight to blame for the excesses of those who treat Shakespeare's plays as 'extended metaphors' or 'dramatic poems' and ignore the fact that they were written for the stage and cannot be understood unless we treat them as such. Northrop Frye is one of the first critical minds of our time, even though I regard his ideal of criticism as a science as a delusion and one which has had a pernicious influence on those he has influenced. But for the purposes of a comic narrative poem, a great figure makes for better and more dramatic effect than a crowd of *epigoni*, and makes the point against the latter more forcibly. There is not much to be said in defence of the psychoanalytic, the social-realist or the mythopoeic schools of literary explication and I attack these critics in their own right as I do those such as Allen Tate and T. R. Henn who appear mainly to be using poetry to exploit their own sensibilities, and those, like Kenneth Burke, who pretend to talk about the style of great writers without showing any trace of it in their own writing. Yet even Blackmur often talks sense in his elephantine way and none of the objects of my satire has attained the eminence which made it worth while to pick him out without positive virtues and achievements which it would be foolish to deny. But it is not to the purpose of satire to admit or consider this. Its purpose is, by isolating and making it ridiculous, to put in a clear light the perversity of judgment and the lapses of sense from which the greatest wits are not immune and which may be concealed from themselves and others precisely because of their eminence in other respects. Its purpose is not to deny, even by implication, their real merits and achievements but to laugh them out of the follies which corrode the virtue of these achievements. The child in Hans Andersen's fable did not deny that the emperor really was an emperor, he simply pointed out that he and his courtiers were deluding themselves about the emperor's clothes.

With the hero of my poem I have proceeded in much the same way as with the eminent critics of England and America. The figure presented for the reader's amusement is in no sense a portrait of the man who has contributed so much to the just and discerning assessment of Australian literature, to mention only the field in which his work is best known today. In the form of deliberate caricature such as the political cartoonist has licence to create, he presents my view of the sort of critical mind which is so set in the romantic view of poetry that it can perpetrate the monstrous absurdity of affirming that Pope was no poet at all. In the same way the figure of Dr Leavis stands for the sort of mind in general which, by taking a narrow view based on one sort of poetry, can fail to see that there are many sorts of poetry and so dismiss a work like *Paradise Lost* out of hand. In the case of Mr Phillips I have not attempted to present my hero as the eponymous figure of a living school of critics, since his cause is in fact an unpopular one today, but as the representative of an older body of critical opinion, which today is being supplanted by richer and more luxuriant absurdities. But, in a sense, they are all tarred with the same brush: they all represent a constant failing of the academic critic: to think he stands above the storm, to regard his role in dealing with the greater and the lesser works of human genius as that of judge and not, as it should be, that of Jacob wrestling for his soul with the angel. Having spent most of my life in this academic pursuit, I suppose that in the last resort my poem is the protest of a poet against the arrogance of the professor who shares his body.

I began by saying that I think of the poem as something of a museum piece. It was written in 1950, and since then the climate of criticism has changed very much and mine is only one among many voices of protest now raised among the academics themselves against the limitations and excesses of the new criticism. Although the two books of funeral games were composed much later, I have tried to confine myself mainly to critical writing which was then a matter of discussion, so that the whole would be 'in period'. In fact most of my examples come from a single collection of essays, *The Critical Spectrum*, edited by G. J. Goldberg and N. M. Goldberg (Englewood Cliffs, 1962) and largely confined to criticism published between 1920 and 1950.

*Canberra 1970*                                    A. D. HOPE

# CONTENTS

*To the Memory*
*of the late Ambrose Philips, esquire and*
*the somewhat later Arthur Angell Phillips, esquire,*
*the onlie begetters*
*of these ensuing verses*

True Hope is swift, and flies with swallow's wings;
Kings it makes gods, and meaner creatures Kings!

# FOREWORD

## by Ambrose Philips

As Mr Pope's *Dunciad* was a true Epick Poem, comparable in all things but length to the *Iliads* of Homer, not indeed giving the whole War of the Dunces but an episode in which the whole is figured, so this *Little Dunciad* is a sort of Odyssey; for in it a hero famous for his wiles and cunning is depicted returning to his kingdom after innumerable sufferings.

The occasion of our author's beginning this poem was an aerial talk or declamation given by my great descendant, in which he shamelessly and sublimely abused Mr Pope, in imitation of the heroes of the *Dunciad* themselves. Upon his demanding an epick to celebrate this act of folly our author was good enough to oblige him with one, together with all those additions, embellishments and imitative adornments customary in the Mock-heroic style. The character of the hero you will find very speakingly drawn and as true to life as a strict deference to the rules of Aristotle would admit; for he thought some enlargement of common stature necessary in the hero of a great action. In all things our author hath first followed Homer and though they be closely adapted to the subject, yet it will not be hard for the reader to discern the episodes of the Council of Immortals, the Journey to the Land of the Dead, the Island of Calypso, the Warning of Nausicaa, the Return of Ulysses and the Slaughter of the Suitors, all taken from the *Odyssey*. From the *Iliad* he hath drawn on the description of the shield of Achilles, the funeral games, the catalogue of the ships and some scenes of battle. Nor has later epick been neglected: like Virgil's, our hero wandering on foreign shores is succoured by the arts of a divine mother, and sent to found a new empire—albeit the tender passions touch him not—like Milton's hero, though fallen, he hopes yet to prevail against the light. And many an happy phrase and many a delightful stroke of wit has been imitated from these and other mighty works of genius that nothing might be omitted such as pertaineth to the True Sublime as it is illustrated in the works of Mr Dryden and of Mr Pope. Indeed, I might almost say of it what Aelius Donatus in his commentary saith of the *Aeneid* of Virgil:

argumentum varium ac multiplex et quasi amborum Homeri carminum instar. praeterea nominibus ac rebus Graecis Latinisque commune et in quo, quod maxime studebat, Romanae simul urbis et Augusti origo contineretur.

For you have but to read Duncedom for *Romanae urbis* and for *Augusti*, Great Arthur, which it is allowable in this species of poesy to do, and the similitude holds in all particulars.

Alas, my great-great-grandson informs me that such is the prevailing ignorance of poetry in the present age—to say nothing of the neglect of learning—that few will recognize the more recondite beauties of our author's work. It has therefore been a labour of love for us both to add those footnotes with which the present text is enriched. It has not been needful, moreover, for us to write these notes ourselves—a thing indeed impossible for those no longer alive—such is the ingenuity of our author that he hath been able to reconstruct from a few poor remains of our critical writings, as from some prediluvian arsebone whole monsters may be guessed, all that we would severally have said upon these subjects; and he hath even added those little touches of Nature, such as the bickerings of successive editors, which it is an art beyond art to attain.

A. P.

# THE ARGUMENT

## Book I

The proposition, the invocation and the inscription—the state of the immortals described—a council in heaven—a messenger of the Goddess Dullness arrives—his dress and way of life described—he claims the throne of Dullness for A. A. Phillips in succession to Ambrose Philips and to that end begs him a place in the *Dunciad*—the immortals demur but ask to hear the story of the hero—a full and moving account of the inhabitants of New Holland, their history, manners, society, learning and literature—the hero's parts, profession and his chance discovery of his pedigree described—his lament at his exiled state—his situation compared with that of Ulysses on the island of Ogygia.

## Book II

The Goddess Dullness perceives his plight and flies to New Holland to aid him—the radio described—the Goddess rouses the Minister for Posts and Telegraphs—visits her son and predicts his future fame—his broadcast talk described and its effect upon the inhabitants of New Holland—the immortals debate his claim—a banquet in heaven with a disquisition on celestial digestion.

## Book III

The banquet in heaven concluded—the messenger invited to relate a genealogy of the hero—a visit to the dead described, followed by the subsequent history of the War with the Dunces—the state of modern learning and criticism described —the hero's claim reasserted and the debate in heaven resumed —the nature and function of satire described and defended— the hero's prayer is answered and his instant apotheosis commanded.

## Book IV

The Herald makes his report to the Goddess Dullness and urges haste in Arthur's apotheosis—the Goddess reveals that his elevation to the throne is only a feint to deceive her enemies—she reveals her darker purpose and decrees the Funeral Games—the new critics are summoned and addressed by the Goddess.

## Book V

The Funeral Games described—the contests of the critics end with the arrival of the super-critic of the new order—the Goddess awards him the prize and orders Arthur's elevation to the throne.

## Book VI

The apotheosis of the hero prepared—his investiture—his slaying of the rival suitors—his sacrifice and prayer and his assumption to the Kingdom of the ghostly Dunces—his flight, his arrival and welcome from man and beast—he utters an oracle—he takes his seat upon the throne of his ancestors—the beginning of his reign described.

# BOOK I

The long-lost Heir of Dullness found, the king
Of pedants at long last restored, I sing:
Relate Thalia, aided by divine
Calliope, how ignorant of his line
And doubly exiled in the Southern Seas
(For the Muse, too, has her Antipodes)
Among the upside-down-men and their arts
He lived; his lineage tell; the pregnant parts
By which he rose—how yet a fool to fame
10   He learned at last his pedigree and name;
Next, how, by native cunning (and divine
Impulsion), he evolved his Grand Design;
Last by what impudence he rose to his
Much meditated apotheosis,
Made his great fore-bear's ridicule his own
And took his seat upon the Sable Throne.

O thou, whatever title please thee best,
Poet or Moralist or Prince of Jest,
Homer's Translator, St John's better part
20   The Lash of Pedants or the Shield of Art,
Or English Horace, or great Dryden's heir,
Immortal Pope, receive from us, whose care

16   the Sable Throne: in the *Dunciad* (IV, 629), the seat of primeval
Chaos. Our author has made it the Throne of Dullness, for in-
deed dullness regnant is anarchy. (A.P.)

19   St John's better part: Viscount Bolingbroke is said to have pro-
vided Mr Pope with the philosophy of the *Essay on Man*. It was
from this poem that my great-grandson chose the specimen of
Mr Pope's work by which he condemned all, ignoring both the
poet and the philosopher. (A.P.)

In these last years of the romantic storm
It is to keep the classic muses warm,
Upon thine altar, roasted whole and fat,
Prime in his folly, and self-slain at that,
Of all the victims dear to ridicule
Thy favourite—a critic and a fool:
Take him; and, as thy habit was, we pray,
30    Share him with Swift and Arbuthnot and Gay!

Immortal souls that walk on asphodel
Have the same privilege lovers know in hell:
To immortality they may commend
One whom they loved, a mistress or a friend.
And so in death Swift's mighty ghost, they say
Chose Arbuthnot—providing Pope chose Gay;
For neither could, by right of genius, come
Though almost winning to Elysium.
There the four friends, as often in their lives,
40    Uncumbered or by mistresses or wives,
Meet still to dine and talk and rhyme and sit
Long over wines that sparkle like their wit.
In old madeira or in mellower port
The Battle with the Dunces is refought;

There the great heroes of the human mind
Are entertained and ancient genius dined;
There Homer will relax, and with a third
Great bumper some lost epic may be heard;
And there, while Horace laughing fills his glass,

32    the same privilege: see Dante, *Inferno*, Canto V.
Not a privilege at all! Lovers were condemned together for
participating in the same sin. (A.A.P.)
Perhaps they *felt* it a privilege, even in Hell, to be together. (A.P.)
43    madeira . . . port: not sparkling wines! (A.P.)
You've got him there, grandad! (A.A.P.)

50    Dyspeptic Virgil lets the bottle pass.

In 1950, at the first full moon
After All Fools' Day in the afternoon
The four immortals, having met and dined,
Were laughing at some sample verse consigned,
As each ten years the custom is, to show
The state of letters in the world below:
Verse without number, statement void of sense
Flat verbiage and verbal flatulence,
Called *Four Quartets*, it kept no time or tune.
60    Pope thought it a political lampoon
Writ by some parson much bemused in beer;
Arbuthnot thought a Bedlam sonneteer;
Swift looked and frowned, and looked and laughed again;
'God help us all!' he said, 'The thing is plain:
Yahoos at last have learned to hold a pen—
This is a *Yahoo Eclogue*, gentlemen.
Go, Gay, and see! There's someone at the gate.'
For at that moment, drowning all debate
And stupefying heaven with its roar,
70    Dull, yet tremendous at the postern-door
Or Tradesmen's Entrance to Elysium,
Thrice Fame's Posterior Trumpet struck them dumb.

50    Dyspeptic Virgil: he made this up! (A.A.P.)
      Not so, son; taken from an old tradition: 'nam plerumque a
      stomacho et a faucibus ac dolore capitis laborabat . . . cibi vinique
      minimi'. (Donatus, *Life of Virgil*) (A.P.)
51–2  How can one date this poem? The broadcast was given on 4
      January (too early). All Fools' Day is 1 April: first full moon,
      3 April (too late). Very inconsiderate of authors to be so inexact.
      Unfair to editors! (A.A.P.)
      Pish! (A.P.)
66    I have perused the work. I can hardly believe it an eclogue but
      from internal evidence I conclude that its author, a Mr T. S.
      Eliot, is in Holy orders, which agrees best with Mr Pope's con-
      jecture. (A.P.)
      Holy disorders! (A.A.P.)

Off went obliging Gay and in a trice
Was back with serious face and twinkling eyes:
'A Herald, sent from the Umbrageous Queen,
The Goddess Dullness, gorgeously obscene,
Impudent, pompous now at heaven's back-door
Demands a parley by the rules of war:
It seems, some madman rushing on his fate
80    Abusing wit two hundred years too late,
And claiming Namby-Pamby for his dad
Wants Pope to put him in the *Dunciad.*
The goddess intercedes on his behalf.'

'I vote,' said Swift, 'we hear him—for the laugh!
And on no other terms can we admit
Her oafish angel to the heaven of wit.
Homer may be allowed his nod, 'tis true,
And Milton's seventh book a yawn or two:
They being so great, could stretch, though none may break,
90    That single law which Art and Nature make

75    Umbrageous Queen: our author presumably means 'shady queen'.
Why not say so, then, instead of using the hideous phrase 'um-
brageous queen'? (A.A.P.)
Such criticism was typical of my grandson's broadcast. (A.P.)
79    That's me! (A.A.P.)
80    And that is I. (A.P.)
Absolutely false that I claimed him as my dad! I may not be
able to read but I *can* count. (A.A.P.)
I was about to add, son, that Namby-Pamby was the name given
me by Mr Pope's friends. (A.P.)
87    Pope: *Essay on Criticism,* 179-80:
    Those oft are stratagems which errors seem
    Nor is it Homer nods but we that dream. (A.P.)
90    What law is this? I never heard of it! (A.A.P.)
If you had read a few lines further in the *Essay on Man,* son, when
preparing to dismiss the whole of Pope on the strength of four-
teen lines you would have come on this:
    All Nature is but art, unknown to thee
    All chance, direction which thou canst not see.
which has the appearance of having been writ with your criticism
in mind. (A.P.)

By which all dullness once it pass this door
Dissolves in laughter and is seen no more.
But ridicule which kills a fool, can serve
His fatuous stare in amber to preserve,
And satire keep the ancient shapes of Vice
Like shaggy monsters in Siberian ice—
Embalmed in laughter, like a jellied eel,
Go, bid Sir Nonsense, then his cause reveal!'

Gay trotted off and presently came back
100    Leading an old, tired academic hack:
For thirty years he had gone round and round
The same dull plot of literary ground,
Lectured on every author by the clock
And minced each poet fine upon his block,
Had served alike Grub-street and Helicon
Till judgment and discernment both were gone,
The Muses' Mountain and the Dunces' Camp
Trod down at last into one pathless swamp—
Not without parts and promise in his time,
110    But each year sinking deeper in the slime;
Like one that gathers duck-weed—dreadful trade!—
Drowned in the general slush himself has made.

Now bumptious in the service of his queen
See him a herald and a go-between!
Half-proud, half-shamefast, in a livery
Of all the sad waste-paper, cap-a-pie

111    This reminds me of something: I smell a plagiarism. (A.A.P.)
Not plagiarism, son, you seem to be ignorant of the older forms
of poetry. Our author aims at Shakespeare's
        half way down
    Hangs one that gathers samphire, dreadful trade.
                (*King Lear*, Act 4, sc. 6)
The Herald, being more than half-way down—but why should
I explain? I shall point out some other parallels so that you may
learn for yourself the art of the mock heroick style. (A.P.)

With which the poor unnecessary zed
Contrived on earth to live and earn his bread:
The flat, sour thesis and the rancid note
120   Formed the chief stuff of this fantastic coat;
Bilgewater Treatise, books of hints and rules
Or plays castrated for the use of schools,
*New Light on Tupper, Key to Henry James,*
Exposure of Bill Wordsworth's little games,
Chit-chat on authors, *Idlings with the Muse,*
White-washing essays, blackguardly reviews,
Anthologies, concordances to Crabbe—
Thrown off to make his gruel thick and slab;
Such was his costume, such he seemed to view!
130   Yet he spoke native English and he knew
Himself now fallen; at the worst he had
Some power to distinguish good from bad,
To know authentic genius when it comes
If only by the pricking of his thumbs.

The air of heaven, for a little space
Revived these dim intuitings of grace;

---

117   *King Lear*, Act 2, sc. 2, Kent to the Herald (this should give you
the idea, son):
      'Thou whoreson zed! Thou unnecessary letter!' (A.P.)

121   Bilgewater Treatise: the Bridgewater Treatises, I suppose, but I
don't see the connection. (A.A.P.)
I assume, son, that, as they attempted to bolster up religion by
the evidence of geology, anatomy and other natural sciences, our
author is here referring to the modern habit of attempting to
bolster poetry with psychology, anthropology, sociology and
other sciences. He had Dr I. A. Richards and others of his kidney
in mind, perhaps. (A.P.)

128,   Surely a fault in our author to compare the messenger with
131,   Beëlzebub in *Paradise Lost* and the witches in *Macbeth*! (A.A.P.)
134   Aha! You see, son, the idea is soon picked up! (A.P.)
Yes, but how can genius be compared with Macbeth? Macbeth
was a murderer. (A.A.P.)
'Macbeth hath murdered sleep!', son! Like genius he is the enemy
of dullness. Could this be our author's meaning? (A.P.)

The four immortals with some pity see
Him blushing, tongue-tied, trembling at the knee.
'Pray take a chair!' says Pope. 'You seem to puff;
140    The roads of Dullness are both long and rough;
Before we hear you, drink a glass of wine!'

'Alas, I dare not, for like Prosperpine
If aught I taste here—so the edict runs
By which the Milky Mothers rule their sons—
These clothes, the only things I have to wear
Will all drop off and vanish back to air.
Then naked I must speak my naked mind,
And, seeing, no more in blindness lead the blind,
Or, worse, say only what is mine to say
150    Which takes my occupation clean away.'

'Well, sir,' growls Swift then, pulling out his watch,
'You know best; come! Your business, and dispatch!'
And pausing to collect his wits a span
The Mighty Mother's envoy thus began:

'Dullness Divine, who still extends her sway,
Whom earth, and on occasion, heaven, obey
Since Theobald was deposed, and Cibber, dead
Like King Pandion, has been lapped in lead,
Mourns that for two full centuries at least
160    No King of critics who was quite a beast
Has ruled the Dunces, and the Sable Throne

144,   Milky Mothers . . . Mighty Mother: who are all these mothers,
154   grandad? (A.A.P.)
     Not to be confused, son! *Alma mater* is a university: *Magna*
     *Mater* is the primeval goddess of Dullness in Mr Pope's *Dunciad*.
     Our author intends the distinction between them to be as wide as
     that between the *dura mater* and the *pia mater* in anatomy. The
     relation of each to the brain of a fool is in fact very similar. (A.P.)
157   Mr Theobald, a pedant, was the first hero of Mr Pope's *Dunciad*,
     but in the second version his place was taken by Mr Cibber, an
     actor. (A.P.)

No Bums of the old Royal Line has known.
Now, in the arsy-versy hemisphere,
Their great-great-great-great-grandsons reappear;
Among them one whose solid ivory skull
Proclaims him royal and confirms him dull,
Whose breadth of fundament and name declare
Him mighty Namby-Pamby's lineal heir;
And him the goddess finds in all things meet
170  To drowse and drool on regal Colley's seat.
But—here's the catch—to make his title good
'Tis not enough to show his royal blood:
His patent must be proved; in fact, the lad
Must get a mention in the *Dunciad*.
And to this end he made, not two months back
A ribald, foolish, unprovoked attack
On Pope, his wit, his morals and his muse
Before the whole great nation of Yahoos;
Denied your genius, sir; your diction found
180  Inadequate and grammar *most* unsound;
And like Tremendous Dennis, proved that he
Saw nothing but what any fool could see;
That exquisite and pure melodic line
Of verse entirely missed, or by design
Ignored; denied its wit and tact and grace;
And gave a lesser poet pride of place;

168  lineal heir: how could this affect the matter? My grandad never
sat on the throne. (A.A.P.)
A consequence of an ancient prophecy, son, which I inherited
from the worthy Banquo. See Book V of the present poem. (A.P.)
178  Yahoos: the land of Yahoos according to Lemuel Gulliver's chart
would lie somewhere in the southern portion of New Holland:
about the region of Lake Eyre, according to some authorities.
(A.P.)
181  And like Tremendous Dennis: Dennis, caricatured by Mr Pope
and his friends as Sir Tremendous in *Three Hours after Marriage*.
Dennis, like my grandson, was determined to see nothing good
in Pope's poetry but 'his knack at smooth verse'. (A.P.)
186  a lesser poet: a Mr John Keats. He hath writ a pretty ode upon
a nightingale. My grandson can speak of nothing else. (A.P.)

Yet showed, as fools turned critics often do,
The sense of what he praised escaped him too.
Such is his claim! The goddess has agreed
190    To back it: In perverted taste, indeed,
Such were his ancestors in former days:
Smug when they snarled and pointless in their praise.
So Circe's swine preferred their beastly mast,
So dogs to their own vomit turn at last,
So carrion-feeders plump for putrid meat
And human jackals care not what they eat,
Their stomachs spoiled by what they shovel in,
Their palates ruined with synthetic gin,
Call the food tasteless when asked out to dine,
200    And, smoking foul mundungus, blame the wine.'

This said he paused and waited their reply.
The four looked grave, then doubtful, and then sly:
'Is it permitted, then,' said Swift, 'to know
What name the hero has with men below?'

'Three names of power,' the answer came, 'he bears:
*Phillips*, in simple majesty declares
Him scion of the Namby-Pamby strain:
*Arthur*, in token he should come again;
These two by mortal kith and kin were given,
210    But *Angel* was the irony of Heaven!'
He ceased; and mock amazement held them fast.
'The case is difficult,' said Pope at last,
'The man's a dunce—we make no bones of that—

192    Our author here seems to echo the words of Mr Pope in his imita-
tion of the first epistle of the second book of Horace:
      A vile encomium doubly ridicules;
      There's nothing blackens like the ink of fools. (A.P.)
208    Arthur, in token: of his great namesake Sir Thomas Malory has
observed: 'But many men say that there is written upon his
tombe this verse: "Hic jacet Arthurus, rex quondam, rexque
futurus." ' (A.P.)

Yet when the Curst Queen pleads, I smell a rat;
When the old Harpy offers gifts at all
Some Wooden Ass she pushes towards the wall;
And put him in the *Dunciad*! My good sir,
I must and shall know more: unless I err,
This plan to make Mad Jack ridiculous
220 Conceals another, to make fools of us.
Yet, if no treachery you contemplate,
Know that an *epic* hero must be great:
To be a fool, and be by fools begot,
And talk much nonsense is man's common lot;
He who to epic folly would attain
Must show himself an ass in Ercles' vein;
And he who would with ancient dullness vie
Achieve some stroke of high absurdity,
"A part to tear a cat in, make all split"—
230 No other can my Dunciad admit.

On either count, then, the whole truth declare!
In every detail, Herald, have a care!
If the least fib you utter, sir, reflect
It lies not in our power to protect:
You perish! For the least omission made,
Or the half-truth so frequent in your trade,
No more the tender goslings round your feet
Shall gobble up your notes like mildewed wheat;
Farewell the lecture-hall's congenial roar!

215–16   some Wooden Ass: what does this mean, grandad? (A.A.P.)
Our author here, son, draws a sublime similitude with the situation described by Virgil, *Aeneid*, II, 48–9:
equo ne credite, Teucri!
quidquid id est, timeo Danaos et dona ferentes. (A.P.)
222–30   an *epic* hero:   our author here has Mr Pope be mindful of Aristotle's rule in his *Poetics* and illustrate it by Shakespeare's admirable practice in the Translation of Bottom. It was in part my neglect of this rule which earned me the title of Namby-Pamby. My descendant, happily, was of more rugged mould. (A.P.)

240   Black-board and chalk shall know your scrawl no more:
Satire, which now protects you, while we please,
Explodes you like a bubble or a sneeze!'

'O sirs!' replied the Herald, 'Have no fear!
Of lie or stratagem this breast is clear;
Great Arthur's story, when it shall be told,
Proves him a numskull of heroic mould,
A tyger's heart wrapt in an asses skin,
Dauntless and dumb—But since I may begin
Hear now the saga of his Grand Design:

250   Far in the South, beyond the burning line,
Where Gulliver that much-wrecked mariner
Described their customs, such as then they were,
And found them, like their manners, somewhat coarse,
The Yahoos live in slavery to the horse.
And since, though little altered from that time,
Great Britain gave them trade and beer and crime
And politics and healthy out-door games,
Now they wear clothes, and some can write their names.
A sort of costive English, too, they speak,
260   And sweat and drink and quarrel round the week;
And what they earn in their own time, they spend
On their four-footed masters each week-end.
As for their arts—the land to you would seem,
O Sirs, like satire's paradisal dream!

247   tyger's heart: is this a quotation, Uncle Namby? (A.A.P.)
Yes, son—almost! Our author here recalls the address of the
noble Duke of York to Queen Margaret in Shakespeare's *King
Henry VI*:
    She-wolf of France, but worse than wolves of France
    Whose tongue more poisons than the adder's tooth . . .
    O tyger's heart wrapt in a woman's hide.
which lines Robert Greene applied to Shakespeare himself:
    His Tygers hart wrapt in a Player's hide.
And all this wealth of obloquy you now inherit, my boy. (A.P.)

As their first simple stockmen, we are told
Pastured their flocks upon a hill of gold,
Beneath an endless, empty, arid plain
The mind's uncharted virgin steppes inane,
Treasures of undiscovered laughter lie
270    And whole Golcondas of stupidity.
Grim civil wars their hapless scribblers wage:
There native frogs with foreign mice engage
And True-born Bandicoots with squeaks protest
Th' imported Rabbit drives them from the nest.
Yet, as of old, marsupial bards abound
And with elastic bounces thump the ground;
And wombat novelists rise, as erst they rose,
To praise their country in illiterate prose.

There the lost heirs of Dullness a whole age
280    Lived unaware of their great heritage;
Among them, even to his peers unknown,
Lived the uncrowned pretender to the throne,
Witless and harmless, and his living made
By plying the bumbaster's tedious trade;
And there, perhaps, would live in ignorance yet,
But that—though how it happened I forget—
I think some idle traffic with the muse—
He chanced one day the *Dunciad* to peruse.

Like Homer's world upon Achilles' shield
290    The World of Dunces stood by art revealed;
With mounting ecstasy he reads, and cries:
"My Native Earth I see, my native skies!"
With stammering lips he read, with eyes that shone,
Spelled out the syllables and, stumbling on,
He found the line: —and shook with sacred rage—
*"She saw slow Philips creep like Tate's poor page."*

295    He found the line: *Dunciad*, I, 105.

Then all made clear, his birth, his pedigree,
"Philips!" he cried, "A. Philips! Why that's ME!
My grandsire (though he only had one L)"
300   (For now the footnote had him in its spell)
"Though I but see thee dark, as in a glass
Oh, tell me now, thou great eponymous ass,
Am I a King, and Dullness' Chosen Lamb?
I feel it in my bones; I know; I *am*!

Yes, such—" he paused, "I should have been, I know:
Vastly pedantic and sublimely low!
But, ah, to woe delivered trussed and bound,
Exiled and orphaned here on alien ground,
Brainless, alone and helpless, here I mourn!
310   How to my Kingdom ever to return?
How prove my title and regain my throne,
Perchance by others claimed ere this, or won?
Ah me, how happy, when unmarked by Fate
I taught the young Yahoos to scrawl and prate,

300   the footnote: I had two mentions in the *Dunciad* in one of which
it is said 'Lo! Ambrose Philips is preferred for wit!' and though
this was said ironically it is, I flatter myself, something to have it
said at all by so eminent an author. Besides this one of my works,
'Thule', was used as fire-extinguisher in the same poem. The
footnote to this incident (Book I) reads: '("Thule") an unfinished
Poem of that name, of which one sheet was printed fifteen Years
ago; by *A. Ph*[ilips] a Northern Author . . . Some Criticks have
been of opinion, that this sheet was of the nature of the *Asbestos*
. . . but I rather think it only an allegorical allusion to the coldness
and heaviness of the writing.' (A.A.P.)
313–23   Our author here seems to touch on the situation of Satan in
*Paradise Lost*, I, 56–62:
         round he throws his baleful eyes
         That witness'd huge affliction and dismay
         Mixt with obdurate pride and stedfast hate:
         At once as far as Angels kenn he views
         The dismal situation waste and wilde
         A Dungeon horrible, on all sides round
         As one great Furnace flam'd . . . (A.P.)

Nor knew myself! Now all the Austral scene,
Race-track, pub, football-ground, poker machine—
Pleasing enough to these Yahoos, perhaps,
To whom all books are made with bets, poor chaps!
Whose height of learning is, at most, the claim
320    To read a jockey's or a horse's name—
But not to me—to me, on all sides round
Cut off from learned duncedom's darling ground,
To me, a dungeon horrible and vile."

So, like Ulysses on Calypso's isle,
Weeping he sat upon that southern shore

And thought to see his native land no more.'

*End of Book I*

# BOOK II

'Through thick and foul, through dark and dusk and dun
The Mighty Mother saw her weeping son;
For Dullness, when her sovereign ease she takes,
Has a celestial thunderbox or jakes
Whose windows serve, like Northern Jove's, to show
All that miscarries in the world below.
From there laborious, busy, bold and blind
She meddles in the muddles of mankind;
And there, in joy reclining to survey
10    Confusion grow to Chaos day by day,
Great Arthur in his doldrums she discerned,
And her heart melted and her bowels yearned.
"Behold!" she cries, "the hundred years are past:
My Prince, my Sleeping Ugly wakes at last!
Of all my poppets, pets, poeticules,
My cretins, critics, philosophs and fools,
Ninnies and zanies, dunderheads and dolts,
Of all that fumbles, dodders, drools and moults
By far the last, the least, the lowest, he
20    Excels my children in fatuity!

4    thunderbox: as in the *Dunciad*, Book II (imitated from Lucian):
        A place there is, betwixt earth, air, and seas
        Where, from Ambrosia, Jove retires for ease. (A.P.)
5    like Northern Jove's: Othin—so in the Edda of Snorri Sturlason:
    'There is a place called Hlithskjalf and when the Allfather [Othin]
    sits on the throne there, then he sees every land and the deeds of
    all men and knows all things that he sees.' (A.P.)
7    laborious, busy, bold and blind: a line so bad that it might
    almost be by Pope himself. (A.A.P.)
    It is, son, it is. (A.P.)

Born for the throne—yet, with his brain how can
He help himself?—I must devise a plan."

Brisk as an ogle darting from a beau
The Goddess dived into the murk below,
And as she plunged, a stratagem she spun
By which she might advance her chosen son.

Now you should know that in this latter age
Men live in their machines as in a cage,
No longer range the woods for roots and nuts
30    But passive, put in their protesting guts
Whate'er their keepers throw them; and their ease
They spend in picking one another's fleas.
This they call Culture, and this word obscene
They worship. In this World of the Machine
No more does genius practise or impart
The selfless, self-absorbed delight of Art:
Vapid and vain, the new men, if you please,
"Engage in Cultural Activities."
Of all the pimps of Culture quite the worst
40    The *Radio* panders to their quenchless thirst
For cheap amusement and degraded wit—
Your faces tell me you have heard of it—
No more then! This mechanical device
The Goddess loves, and in her power it lies:
She chooses its chief slaves with special care—
Now when some Dennis croaks upon the air,
The lie, enlarged till half the nation hears,
Creeps like a louse into a million ears.
And this machine the Goddess had in mind

23–6    So in my own unfinished poem, 'Thule':
Eastward the goddess [June, in this case] guides her gaudy team,
And perfects, as she rides, her forming scheme. (A.P.)

50    As on she flapped and floundered, flying blind,
And felt the rear of Darkness, like her plot,
Thicken, and curdle from her wings and clot.

At last she recognized New Holland's coasts,
And sped to where the Minister for Posts,
Whose charge is to police this dire machine
And keep the waves of aether calm and clean,
Slumbered full length in his baroque bureau
While all his civil service snored below.
The Goddess took the flabby shape and name
60    Of the Nymph Culture—Houses of ill-fame
She keeps, and there by bureaucratic arts
She strives to make the Muses all turn tarts;
No politician can her wiles resist;
Her name is on the Civil Pension's list—
With all *her* unction now the Goddess spoke:
"Awake sweet chuck!"—the Minister awoke,
Said: "Oh, it's you!" and slapped her fair behind,
And fell asleep again. She did not mind:
Such men a Goddess has small cause to fear.
70    She bent and whispered something in his ear.

This done, she flew to where upon the shore
Sad Arthur gnawed what nails he had to gnaw.
In her own shapeless shape the Queen appears
And on her son the Mighty Mother stares:

51-2    felt the rear of Darkness: our author here indicates that Dullness
has the opposite nature from the bird in Milton's
         while the Cock with lively din
            Scatters the rear of darkness thin. (A.P.)
All Greek to me! (A.A.P.)
53ff.    Speaking of the Greek, son, for further instruction in the mock
epick style, you would do well to compare this passage with the
opening of Book VI of the *Odyssey* where Athene, disguised,
rouses the sleeping Nausicaa. (A.P.)

She sees that face as long as a bull's foot,
She marks the sobs of the desponding brute,
His shoes unlaced, his shirt-tails hanging out
And liquid misery dripping from his snout.
"Rise, Owl of Exile! Rise, thou Wandering Star!
80   Thine hour hath struck! Be known for what you are!
Consider the great seed from which you sprung!"
She greeted him; then, tempering her tongue:
"Attend, O child of very little brain,
And listen carefully while I explain
A plot as simple as the A.B.C.
That brings *you* home, and strikes a blow for *me*:
You will receive, within an hour or so,
A sooty Ariel of the radio
Inciting you to arson—and, I hope,
90   To make a bonfire of the works of Pope.
Think not, my bumble-puppy boy, to vie
With Caliph Omar or Chi-Ho-Am-Ti!
They burned whole worlds of learning, it is true:
One work of genius is enough for you.
Go then, blaspheme, be dense, pedantic, crude;
Be sourly funny, oafish, crass and rude!
The fools Pope blasted could not write, indeed;
But you must prove you cannot even read!
In this be counselled: Seek to know no more!
100  For though with dullness rarely seen before,

79   Wandering Star: is not the long lost, late discovered planet
     Pluto, here intended? (A.A.P.)
     It seems apt, indeed. (A.P.)
81   Consider the great seed: cf. Dante, *Inferno*, XXVI, 118–19:
            Considerate la vostra semenza:
            Fatti non foste a vivir come bruti. (A.P.)
90   The title of my broadcast was 'Standard Works I'd Like to Burn:
     Alexander Pope'. (A.A.P.)
     Yes, yes, son! (A.P.)
92   Omar ... Chi-Ho-Am-Ti: famous book-burners: See Mr Pope's
     *Dunciad*, III, 73–82. (A.P.)

Your royal breed yourself you have found out
'Tis mine to bring your sovereign state about.
Do as I bid: Your serendipity
May safely sleep and leave the rest to me!"

This said, a tender kiss her love bestows
Where one lost tear runs trickling down his nose;
Then bursting into soft maternal flame
She vanished and flew back the way she came.

As she had prophesied it all came true:
110    As bold as brass, and twice as brazen too,
Undaunted Arthur moves to his attack
Knowing dead authors never answer back;
From all your works the least superb selects,
And all that shows your genius best rejects;
Chooses "some lines at random"—poor pretence—
Ignores the context and neglects the sense;
Afraid of the attack-in-chief, creeps around
Finds a lame verb, an epithet unsound;
From twenty thousand verses makes a list
120    Of two false forms and seven commas missed—
So the small tyke that fears your boot or whip
Slinks round behind and gives your heels a nip.
As Easter Island savages, who see
The art and wisdom of antiquity
Mouldering on tablets which they cannot read,
And statues which they sell in idle greed,
Turn on the past uncomprehending eyes
And what they cannot understand, despise;
But have the wit to haggle, cheat and steal
130    And pass off bogus carvings for the real,
So Arthur reads your verse: His empty bray
Declares it sense and beauty thrown away,

105–8    Cf. *Aeneid*, I, 402ff. A very beautiful example of our author's
power of compression. (A.P.)

Yet, with the paltry cunning of his kind
Orders the strange vagaries of his mind,
The battered *cliché* and the tawdry trope,
Salts with your verse—and passes it as Pope.

Thus, thus his words on wings of lightning borne,
He strewed like tares amid the alien corn!
Now hear the sequel: Through the listening land
140    Dumb with astonishment the natives stand;
Unlettered lads, with mouths that gape or grin,
They scratch their heads and strive to take it in;
By every hearth some patriarch Yahoo
Cries as the cork pops out of the home-brew,
And from the shelf the Racing News is snatched:
"Well, what d'you know, Mum: bloody Pope's been
    scratched!"

But from on high the Mother Goddess smiled,
And, through proud tears she cried: "Well done, my child!"
Then me she summoned to her awful throne
150    And charged and sent me forth. The rest is known.'

The Herald ceased. 'An epic ass enough
He seems to be—', said Pope, but Swift looked gruff,
Arbuthnot frowned, like Gay, and shook his head.
'I think you should refuse this plea,' he said.
'Such madding fools, to see their names in print
Stick at no crime, in folly know no stint,
Nor infamy distinguish from renown

138    Echo of a line in my grandson's favourite poem. (A.P.)
139-47  These lines, specially inserted by our author at my request, are an
    example of that Bathos or Art of Sinking in poetry for which my
    pastoral style was renowned. Mr Pope himself has given a justly
    celebrated imitation in his essay upon my poetry in the *Guardian*.
    (A.P.)
141    with mouths . . . They scratch: how absurd! How could they
    scratch their heads with their mouths? (A.A.P.)

Like him who burned Diana's temple down;
But few achieve such note in any age;
160   The most run wild at random, wreck and rage
And, would-be dunceling martyrs, try their luck,
Proud to be shot for having run amuck.
Think of *your* dunces! Some whose nameless name
You saved have now achieved a kind of fame,
For Dullness too has her Elysium;
"Martyrs of pies and reliques of the bum",
Such as our sires and we thought best forgot,
Or fit like thorns to crackle neath a pot,
Are now by tasteless scholarship restored
170   And, shrined in gems, exploited and adored:
Your Arthur seems this dangerous kind of Ass
And simulates more folly than he has.'

'Indeed, sir,' answered Gay, 'I find it hard
To think him hoisted with his own petard:
So much an ass for this had not the wit;
'Twas for the guineas, surely, that he writ.'

'Not so!' cried Swift. 'There you mistake him, John!
Knave he may be, but not a venal one.
I know them well, the dogs, at least, I *knew*
180   Those hired bullies of the midnight crew,
Such as beat Dryden and they said—or tried—

158   Like him who burned: Eratostratus who burned the famous and
beautiful temple of Ephesus to have his name remembered. (A.P.)
166   Martyrs of pies...bum: Dryden, *Mac Flecknoe*. See also *Dunciad*,
I, 143–4:
     Here all his suffering brotherhood retire
     And 'scape the martyrdom of jakes and fire. (A.P.)
181–2   Such as beat Dryden...and they said...beat Pope: Dryden is
said to have been waylaid and beaten by bullies—some say at the
command of the Earl of Rochester. Lord Hervey and Lady Mary
W. Montague tried to spread a similar tale about Mr Pope but
the plot misfired. (A.P.)

Beat Pope—but dirty Lady Mary lied!
As Borgia's *bravi* care not whom they drown
And cut a nameless throat for half-a-crown,
The menial Judas, for the higher pay
Will his own Lord or any lord betray,
Kills without question, asks not whom he stabs
And laughing sells his mother or his drabs.
Such rogues shun fame—and there lies proof enough
190    Arthur is made of more ambitious stuff.
No, to my mind, there is no doubt at all
'Tis vanity, not greed hath been his fall.
The lesser critics of the canine kind
Will lift their legs where'er they have a mind
On posts and trees and gates and wheels of carts,
But one, to prove himself a dog of parts,
The common sprinkler of the suburb shuns,
And hoards his drop, and through the town he runs
And all he has bestows with pious care
200    On Caesar's statue in the public square;
Proud to be seen and hear his fellows cry:
"He pissed on Julius Caesar—so will I."
Your Arthur's of this kidney—best refuse
And let the * * * stew in his own juice.'

'Who shall dissent when doctors both agree?'
Replied the poet, 'Yet it seems to me
Something on his behalf may yet be said:
He may yet prove an *honest* mutton-head.
Speaking of mutton, though, have you observed

188    So Dryden, *Absalom and Achitophel*, II, 429:
        For almonds he'll cry whore to his own mother. (A.P.)
205    Pope, Epistle III, iff., *Moral Essays*:
        Who shall decide when doctors disagree
        And soundest casuists doubt, like you and me? (A.P.)

210    That, while we chatted, supper has been served?
     And, shades of Dartineuf! Methinks I spy
     Before us a celestial ham-pye.
     Now, Master Herald, briefly as you can
     Tell us the lineage of your Caliban!
     Can it be proved? For if you can recite
     Each link from Namby-Pamby on, I might—
     Mind, I don't say I shall—I might agree.
     Proceed, then, with his royal pedigree!'
     'Yes, but not now!' cried Swift and Gay distressed.
220    'Let us have supper ere we hear the rest!
     Immortal substance still must be kept up;
     The Messenger may join us while we sup—
     God knows, he's earned at least a glass of wine.'

     'Alas, don't press me, gentlemen, to dine!'
     He said, 'I must refuse, indeed, I must;
     Though sorely tempted—No offence, I trust!'

     'Well here's a pretty pass!' cried Pope. 'We can
     Scarce eat this pye before a starving man.
     'Tis a good dunce—I've dined with many worse;
230    He knows his manners and he *don't* write verse.
     Come, doctor, sure your art must have a rule
     To settle the digestion of a fool!

211   Dartineuf (or Dartiquenave): a famous epicure of my day. Pope,
     *Satire* II, 44–5:    none deny
        Scarsdale his bottle, Darty his ham-pye. (A.P.)
230   Mr Pope was particularly pestered by this type of fool. See
    *Epistle to Dr Arbuthnot*:
        Then from the Mint walks forth the man of rhyme
        Happy to catch me, just at dinner-time.
        Is there a Parson, much be-mused in beer
        A maudlin poetess, a rhyming peer,
        A clerk fore-doomed his father's soul to cross,
        Who pens a stanza when he should engross ... (A.P.)

As Adam found his airy angel guest
Could munch a carrot, taste, concoct, digest
—though there the matter stopped; a good thing, too!—
Say what an ass's mortal paunch can do
With pye ambrosial and immortal hock!
Resolve! Decide! We sup at six o'clock!'
To whom Arbuthnot: 'He need not abjure
240    Our sustenance for food alike these pure
Unthinking substances indeed require
As do our rational: but they perspire
The finer essences, which we retain
(For airy substances turn all to gain);

233-52    Our author here hath imitated that delightful passage of *Paradise Lost*, Book V, in which Adam in doubt invites the angel to partake his vegetable feast and is answered with subtle doctrine:

> To whom the Angel. Therefore what he gives
> (Whose praise be ever sung) to Man in part
> Spiritual, may of purest Spirits be found
> No ingrateful food: and food alike those pure
> Intelligential substances require
> As doth your Rational; and both contain
> Within them every lower facultie
> Of sense, whereby they hear, see, smell, touch, taste,
> Tasting concoct, digest, assimilate
> And corporeal to incorporeal turn.
> For know, whatever was created, needs
> To be sustained and fed; of Elements
> The grosser feeds the purer, Earth the Sea,
> Earth and the Sea feed Air, the Air those Fires
> Ethereal, and as Lowest First the Moon;
> Whence in her visage round those spots, unpurgd
> Vapours not yet into her substance turnd . . .
> The Sun that light imparts to all, receives
> From all his alimental recompence
> In humid exhalations, and at Even
> Sups with the Ocean.

The like subtle and difficult question hath been answered by our author in a disquisition not devoid of allegory. (A.P.)

I think it all in very poor taste: as I did the passage in Pope's *Essay on Man* where he represents Nature suckling the flowers. (A.A.P.)

And thus our guest may sup with us today,
Provided only he prolong his stay
Till the immortal part, which is less dense,
From all his alimental recompense
In humid exhalations vanish soon;
250    Nor suffer indigestion like the moon—
Go read it all in Milton, if you will!
Besides, if Nature fails, I have a pill.'

'Come, Sir,' said Swift, 'be easy! Supper waits.'

So all sat down in peace and filled their plates.


## End of Book II

# BOOK III

Their supper ended, round the board they sit
While ease and laughter feed the flame of wit.
And now the covers drawn, each glass returned,
Clear in that windless dusk the candles burned,
The crystal glittered and the silver shone
The wine went round, the flow of talk swept on;
Till, the first stars emerging, grave and dim,
Far off the Muses raised their evening hymn,
Intent, in heavenly silence, rapt, profound,
10   All heard that solemn, pure, rejoicing sound
Sweetness and light in all the earth proclaim
And light and order in the starry frame.

How long they might have sat I cannot tell,
For suddenly the Herald broke the spell
With: 'Charming! Charming! Thank you, gentlemen!
But now I must take up my tale again.

What proof, you ask, attests the hero's claim
Beside his bearing of the family name?
This, too, the Mighty Mother took in hand
20   And, on my setting forth, she gave command:
"Ere Arthur to his Kingdom may return

---

11-12   Sweetness and light: cf. 'As for us the ancients . . . we have
rather chosen to fill our hives with honey and wax; thus furnish-
ing mankind with the two noblest of things which are sweetness
and light.' (Swift, *The Battle of the Books*) (A.P.)
21-2   Thus the Shade of Anchises to Aeneas (*Aeneid*, V, 730ff.):
        gens dura atque aspera cultu
Debellanda tibi Latio est. Ditis tamen ante
Infernas accede domos, et Averna per alta
Congressus pete, nate, meos . . .
Tum genus omne tuum, et, quae dentur moenia, disces. (A.P.)

He from the dead his pedigree must learn:
But since, dear lad, he's sure to garble it,
Some proxy more endowed with mother-wit
Must take his place. That proxy, sir, is you!
Attend, while I explain what is to do:

Before you journey to Elysium
To Arthur's land of exile must you come.
At the world's end, on mud that never dries
30    For the sun rarely shines, that city lies,
Sunday's necropolis laid out in squares
And sacred to the Whig whose name it bears,
My quondam Lamb whose name was writ on silt,
And there a three-fold mortuary is built
Where books and bones and canvas rest in peace.
These three museums seek! In one of these
Old Masters, many genuine, are hung;
In one a dead gorilla shows its tongue,
And there the idol the Yahoos adore,
40    The Sacred Racehorse stuffed with manger-straw
Stands in his case and winks a glassy eye—
These two in pious dread you must pass by;
The third grim catacomb or cenotaph,
Holds all the dead dull critics bound in calf.
The powder of oblivion drifting down
Covers the ignorant sneer, the pompous frown.

30ff.    What place is this, son, and why is it called necropolis? (A.P.)
        Melbourne, grandad, because so dead on a Sunday. (A.A.P.)
34ff.    The former Melbourne Public Library, Art Gallery and Museum.
        Our author here imitates the description of the Temple of Apollo.
        (*Aeneid*, VI, 13ff.) (A.A.P.)
40ff.    The Sacred Racehorse: 'Veneris monimenta nefandae'? (A.P.)
        No, grandad, the stuffed skin of the racehorse *Phar Lap*, wor-
        shipped by the natives of New Holland! (A.A.P.)

This is your goal. Now mark me well: you must
First dig a trench in that millennial dust,
And thrice curse Pope, and thrice in holy fear,
50  Summon the ghostly Dunces to appear.
Straight they will come in myriads at your call;
Then three drops from your fountain pen let fall
Into the trench; the black, pedantic ink
Let Dennis first, then Namby-Pamby drink,
Then Theobald—and bid each his offspring tell,
And keep the tally as they rise from Hell.
Last, write it down and find ere you depart
Arthur; and see he learns it all by heart.
When all is done, towards Heaven make your way
60  And ask a parley of the sons of day."

I have that paper here: you may peruse
The list at leisure, sir; I would not choose
To give you the whole grisly catalogue,

47ff.   Cf. *Odyssey* (Pope's translation), Book X and Book XI:
Here opened hell, all hell I here implored
And from the scabbard drew the shining sword:
And trenching the black earth on every side,
A cavern formed, a cubit long and wide . . .
Thus solemn rites and holy vows we paid
To all the phantom-nations of the dead;
Then died the sheep: a purple torrent flowed
And all the caverns smoked with steaming blood
When lo! appeared along the dusky coasts
Thin, airy shoals of visionary ghosts.

53ff.   The sacred draught shall all the dead forbear,
Till awful from the shades arise the seer.
Let him, oraculous, the end, the way,
The turns of all thy future fate display,
Thy pilgrimage to come, and remnant of thy day.
(ibid., X, 640ff.)

55   bid each his offspring tell: so *Aeneid*, VI, 752ff.:
Nunc age, Dardaniam prolem quae deinde sequatur
Gloria, qui maneant Itala de gente nepotes
Inlustres animas nostrumque in nomen ituras,
Expediam dictis, et te tua fata docebo. (A.P.)

Each puddle of the vast Serbonian bog.
As if a Hogarth's pencil had designed
This long Rake's Progress of the human mind,
All my endeavour is by steps to trace
Him still descending from the Dunciad race;
For without raking the whole noisome midden he
70    Can still be proved a hero of their kidney.

Well to begin, and add worse things to bad:
For fifty years after your Dunciad
This noble, passionate, lucid verse we saw
Impose its beauty and declare its law;
The fools were silenced and the rogues sat mum;
The venal, vicious oracles were dumb;
For fifty years that blaze of grace and light
Though dwindling, kept the creatures out of sight.
Yet, as the sun receded, underground
80    The old malicious gossip went the round;
Still the lie festered and the rumour spread
Where in the dark they gnawed and squeaked and bred,
Till with a rush at last they left their holes
Pushing in front the Reverend Billy Bowles.

64    Each puddle: so *Paradise Lost*, II, 592–4:
        A gulf profound as that Serbonian Bog
        Betwixt Damiata and mount Casius old,
        Where Armies whole have sunk. (A.P.)

84    Billy Bowles: the Reverend William Lisle Bowles published an
edition of the *Works* of Pope in 1806. It was Bowles who spread
the cant about Pope which I did no more than repeat in my
broadcast (with the difference that I allowed him no merit what-
ever), viz. that Pope is artificial, smooth and lacking the qualities
of the highest sort of poetry: e.g.: 'All Pope's successful labour
of correct and musical versification, all his talents of accurate
description, though in an inferior province of poetry'. (Preface
to 1806 edition.)

    This Preface led to a famous quarrel—Byron attacked it in
*English Bards and Scotch Reviewers*—Campbell championed Pope
—Bowles replied with his *Invariable Principles of Poetry* (1819) and
so the great battle as to whether Pope was a poet or not began
and has continued to this day. (A.A.P.)

Like fatuous Warton, even in your time
Moaning: "Pope not Pathetick, not Sublime!"
Officious Billy, called to trim the bays,
Coated them with the mildew of his praise:
"Pope not a poet of the Highest Order,
90    All tinsel, tinkle, artifice and solder!"
From there how short the step, how deep the fall
To the next age's: "Pope no poet at all!"

Now open war replaced uneasy truce:
At first they flatter only to traduce;
But soon, these poor pretences thrown away,
The naked ulcers of their hate display.
Then in Pope's cause four mighty champions rose:
The shields of Byron, Campbell interpose,
And sturdy Hazlitt springs to his defence;
100    Behind them Savage Landor looms immense.
Campbell floored Bowles, and Byron's cut-and-thrust

85-90    Like fatuous Warton: Joseph Warton, *Essay on the Genius And
Writings of Pope* (1756): 'I revere the memory of Pope, I respect
and honor his abilities; but I do not think him at the head of
his profession. In other words, in that species of poetry wherein
Pope excelled, he is superior to all mankind and I only say, that
this species of poetry is not the most excellent one of the art . . .
The Sublime and the Pathetick are the two chief nerves of all
genuine poesy. What is there transcendently Sublime or Pathetick
in Pope?' Here Mr Warton seems to me to err only in partiality.
(A.A.P.)

97-8    So Hector in Pope's *Iliad* (Book XIV) when struck down by
Ajax:
                In vain an iron tempest hisses round;
                He lies protected and without a wound.
                Polydamus, Agenor the divine,
                The pious warrior of Anchises' line,
                And each bold leader of the Lycian band,
                With covering shields (a friendly circle) stand.
See also *Paradise Lost*, VI, 335ff. (A.P.)

Slew Southey; hosts of critics bit the dust.
The day seemed won—Alas, day turned to night!
It rained and soon there was no dust to bite:
The climate of the mind at last had changed;
Something in human nature seemed deranged;
Vast fogs of feeling sundered Man from men;
Romantic swamps oozed thickly from the pen;
And now the woolly-witted flocks protest
110    That Pope lacked vegetable interest!
And not alone mere critic foes he had,
But mighty poets in their misery mad:
Wordsworth, the most erected spirit that fell,
Coleridge that wrote the metaphysic of hell,
Though great and gifted joined the general rant,
The cant of Nature and the cant of Kant,
Decried the clear dry light of classic art
Which lacked 'essential passions of the heart'.
"Poet of Reason!" they abused him then—
120    *Poet!* and *Reason!* echoed from the fen.

102    slew Southey: in *English Bards and Scotch Reviewers, A Vision of Judgment, Hints from Horace,* etc. Though not directly involved in this quarrel, Southey did engage in a half-hearted way: 'The age of Pope was the golden age of poets, but it was the pinch beck age of poetry ... the art meanwhile was debased, and it continued to be as long as Pope continued lord of the ascendant.' (*Life of Cowper,* 1819) (A.A.P.)

110    E.g. 'No one can stand pre-eminent as a great Poet, unless he has not only a heart susceptible of the most pathetic or most exalted feelings of Nature, but an eye *attentive to,* and *familiar with,* every change of season, every variation of light and shade, every rock, every tree, every leaf in her solitary places ... Here Pope, from infirmities, and from physical causes was particularly deficient.' W. L. Bowles on his High Horse! (A.A.P.)

113    *Biographia Literaria*—In this work a sort of metaphysic of poetry is attempted which owes much to Kant and his successors in German philosophy. (A.A.P.)

116    the cant of Kant: Coleridge's transcendentalism: see previous note.

119    'because he is always intelligible, it is taken for granted that he is the "Poet of Reason", as if this was a reason for his being no poet.' (Lord Byron, in his very ill-advised defence of Pope.) (A.A.P.)

"Mere metrical good sense!" another cried.
"Mere polish and no sense at all!" replied
De Quincey—"Yet so brilliant, strong and neat—
Yet careless—Pope is *always* counterfeit!—
Yet a great poet with the gift of tongues—
And yet a locomotive with weak lungs!"

So most from their own incoherence burst,
And friends and foes changed sides and praised and cursed.
Next Landor laid the doddering Wordsworth low
130 And all heard Thackeray's jubilant trumpet blow.
New champions rose: though none would treat or yield
At least there seemed the chance of a drawn field.
Then Arnold uttered on the dismal shore

121 'Pope's *Essay on Man* . . . mere metrical good sense and wit'
(Coleridge, *Notes on Selden's Table Talk*) (A.A.P.)

121-6 Nothing but the whole can do justice to De Quincey's sublime
incoherence. The following specimen will give some idea of it:
'I admire Pope in the very highest degree; but I admire him as a
pyrotechnic artist . . . Of all poets who have practised reasoning
in verse, Pope is the one most inconsequential in the deduction of
his thoughts . . . Pope's defect in language . . . lay in an inability,
nursed doubtless by indolence, to carry out and perfect the ex-
pression of the thoughts . . . the short puffs of anger, the uneasy
snorts of fury in Pope's satires give one painfully the feeling of a
locomotive engine with unsound lungs . . . Sudden collapses of
the manufactured wrath . . . announce Pope's as always counter-
feit . . . Not for superior correctness, but for qualities the very
same as belong to his most distinguished brethen is Pope to be
considered a great poet, for impassioned thinking, powerful de-
scription, pathetic reflection, brilliant narration.' (A.A.P.)
The only thing against De Quincey, son, appears to be that he
takes from your attack even the pretence of originality. (A.P.)

129-30 Landor: *Satire on Satirists*, 1836
Thackeray: *The English Humorists*. (A.P.)

133ff. Arnold, *The Study of Poetry* (1880): 'Do you ask me whether
Dryden's verse, take it almost where you will, is not good? . . .
I answer: Admirable for the purpose of the inaugurator of an
age of prose and reason. Do you ask me whether Pope's verse,
take it almost where you will, is not good? . . . I answer:
Admirable for the purposes of the high priest of an age of prose
and reason . . . Dryden and Pope are not classics of our poetry,
they are classics of our prose.' To appreciate cant and nonsense
at the full one should read it all. (A.A.P.)

His melancholy long withdrawing roar:
"Say, do you ask me whether Dryden could
Write verse?—I answer: It is prose and good!
Did Pope, you ask, could *anyone* suppose,
Write poetry? I answer: He wrote prose!
Now, do you ask me whether pigs can fly?

140   No?—Well, no matter! I shall still reply—"
But Tennyson broke in with: "Pope, God bless us!
No human feeling and too many s's!"
Henceforth hemmed in by moonshine, mist and damp,
The cause of Pope was a beleaguered camp.
And so it has continued to this day,
Though still the better critics turn his way
(For still they come, though a diminished band,
And still the watch is kept, the gates are manned
And through the night the crystal ramparts shine)

150   But not through such as these runs Arthur's line.
The road we take now goes from bad to worse:
Our task not now bad critics to rehearse,
Nor tell their numskulls round the charnel-walls—
Now Criticism herself declines and falls!

This maid whom Dryden taught to rule serene
And gave the voice and bearing of a queen,

141-2   'The "Elegy on the Unfortunate Lady" is good, but I do not find
much human feeling in him except perhaps in "Eloisa to Abelard"
... He quoted: *What dire offence from amorous causes springs.*
"Amrus causes springs", horrible! I would sooner die than write
such a line.' (Hallam, Lord Tennyson: *Lord Tennyson: A memoir,*
1897) (A.A.P.)

155   This maid whom Dryden taught: 'Dryden may be properly con-
sidered as the father of English criticism ... The criticism of
Dryden is the criticism of a poet; not a dull collection of theorems,
not a rude detection of faults, which perhaps the censor was not
able to have committed; but a gay and vigorous dissertation,
where delight is mingled with instruction, and where the author
proves his right of judgment, by his power of performance.'
(Samuel Johnson, *Lives of the Poets*)

Whom Johnson taught discriminating praise,
Since Arnold died has come on evil days.
First, falling in with Comus and his train,
160   *Aestheticism* slightly turned her brain;
Crude *Realism* beat her black and blue,
Made her talk cant and spoiled her manners too;
By-ends, the Educator, took her up,
Dosed her with *Culture's* pale, enfeebling cup;
Dull *Social Theory* made her gross and blind;
*Psychology*, afraid to speak her mind;
And worst of all, the old word-eating crew,
Bentleys and Theobalds whom the Dunciad knew
Usurped her function, shared her plundered fame,
170   While *Bibliography* annexed her name.

Now Arnold's nightmare children walk the land;
*Culture* and *Anarchy* go hand in hand:
See scholarship turn a mechanic art
And critics put the horse behind the cart!

163   By-ends, the Educator: I don't understand this obscure jibe.
(A.A.P.)
I think, son, our author intends here, by allusion, the modern
pseudo-science of Education. The character of Mr By-Ends of
Fair-Speech is perhaps not familiar enough to the modern reader:
'*Christian*: Pray, who are your kindred there, if a man may be
so bold?
*By-ends*: Almost the whole Town; and in particular, my Lord
*Turn-about*, my Lord *Time-server*, my Lord *Fair-Speech* (from
whose Ancestors that Town first took its name): Also Mr
*Smooth-man*, Mr *Facing-bothways*, Mr *Anything* and the parson of
our Parish, Mr *Two-tongues*, was my Mother's own Brother by
Father's side: And to tell you the Truth, I am a Gentleman of
good Quality; yet my Great-Grandfather was but a Waterman,
looking one way, and rowing another; and I got most of my
Estate by the same occupation.' (*The Pilgrim's Progress*) Where,
our author contends, could you get a more perfect description of
modern education? (A.P.)

Now in the temple see the hucksters thrive!
When Arnold, Pater, Ruskin were alive
The scholar-critics such as then we had
Were either grandly right or greatly bad
Mighty in judgment, giants when it failed,
180    Round the whole world of letters Raleigh sailed,
A Leslie Stephen, Saintsbury or Ker
Treated it like the conquerors they were.
But since they died their bodies above ground
Lie festering many a rood, and swarming round,
The modern critics of the maggot breed
Writhe in their carcasses and seethe and feed.
Laborious, timid, tedious at once
Each purblind scholar and each well-trained dunce,
From the Old World and from the New they come
190    To rake the rubbish-heaps of Christendom.
Is there a minor poet by others missed
Dull sermoneer or maudlin novelist,
Some corpse to build a reputation on?
A thesis swallows them and they are gone.
Round greater tombs they mine and countermine:
One shrieks: "Stand off, his first ten years are mine!"
"And mine the *floreat!*" Number Two replies;
"Well, then," screams Three, "I've got him till he dies!"
With muck-rake zeal they ferret from the dead
200    All that each genius farted, belched or said;
Flip-flap and fly-leaves, dates and deeds and wills—
They publish everything from midwives' bills
To epitaphs: Whole books grow out of what
His aunts remembered or his dad forgot.

183–4    So Milton of Satan (*Paradise Lost*, I, 194–6):
                his other Parts besides
        Prone on the Flood, extended long and large
        Lay floating many a rood . . . (A.P.)

Columbia, Bates College, Illinois
Receive their quota of the crawly boys;
And some from stranger places still have come,
Kalamazoo, Miami, Muskingum
And Drake and Duke, Sweet Briar and Sacred Word,
210 And seats of learning even more absurd.
There they pupate, and, doctors all, they lurch
Uttering their parrot-cry: Research, Research!
The scabs scratched off by genius, sought with care
Stuck back again earn Doctor Budge a chair;
And now, Professor Budge, his claim made good,
He works like dry-rot through the Sacred Wood;
Or like dead mackerel, in a night of ink
Emits a pale gleam and a mighty stink.
This madness, by the goddess Dullness fanned,
220 Blows the infection on from land to land:

205-10   Our author here, son, imitates the famous Catalogue of the Ships
in Homer (Pope's *Iliad*, Book II):
    O say what heroes, fired by thirst of fame,
    Or urged by wrongs to Troy's destruction came.
    To count them all demands a thousand tongues
    A throat of brass, and adamantine lungs . . .
    The hardy warriors whom Boetia bred
    Penelius, Leitus, Prothoenor, led . . .
    These head the troop that rocky Aulis yields
    And Eteons hills and Hyries watery fields . . .
Like Homer, our author gives pride of place to the Boetian cities.
(A.P.)
Why Boetia, grandad? Boetia is in Greece! (A.A.P.)
! ! ! ! ! ! (A.P.)
214      Doctor Budge: why Budge, grandad? (A.A.P.)
Perhaps a reference to the dictionary will suffice, son. The
*Shorter Oxford* explains: Budge: [? attributive use of Budge sb.[1].
Thus *budge doctor* would be originally one who wore budge fur.]
Solemn in demeanour, pompous, formal . . . 'Those budge doc-
tors of the Stoic Fur.' MILT. *Comus* 707. I own, however, that
our author's meaning here is dark. (A.P.)

Toronto takes the frenzy and McGill,
Mexico City sickens and falls still;
Across the ocean next the morbus flies
And pedantry grows rank as learning dies,
See schools at Oxford stricken don by don
And rabid fluxions seize the whole Sorbonne,
St Andrews feed her sons on mould and fust
And proud Bologna scrabble in the dust,
Uppsala, Padua, Athens and The Hague
230   Proliferate learnèd bumf and boost the plague,
Sources and pointless analogues stuff the trough
For gruntlings from Coimbra to Krakow,
While Heidelberg and Göttingen go down
Seared by "the strong contagion of the gown";
Just doom indeed, for from their halls, 'tis said
At first the strange root-rot infection spread
Which turned the Liberal Arts to factories
For grinding poems down to Ph.Ds.
Nor are those scholiasts able to prevail
240   Who against Notes and Queries hoist their sail.
Dispensing first with facts, with caution next,
They vow a pure devotion to the text;
Prove taste unarmed by scholarship lays waste
More ground than learning innocent of taste.
The Brave New Criticism ends its days
Explaining every context fifty ways.
Leavis, a critic on the Cambridge hearth,

234   contagion of the gown: what disease is this, grandpa? (A.A.P.)
The learned Samuel Johnson, my boy, considering the young
scholar's gown as the shirt of Nessus but for the opposite reason
adopted by our author (*The Vanity of Human Wishes*, II, 135–8):
    When first the college rolls receive his name,
    The young enthusiast quits his ease for fame;
    Through all his veins the Fever of renown
    Burns from the strong contagion of the gown. (A.P.)

Leads his young Mohocks on the scalping path;
But what began as a high-souled crusade
250 Ends in the senseless blood-bath of a raid;
Their Scrutinies on every Muse they turn
And factious in their fury rape and burn;
Their *New Directions* take all roads at once
To end in the blind alleys of the dunce.
Betrayed by one-eyed logic, undeterred
They glory in defence of the absurd
And Milton's hurled to his "bottòmless pit"
While Andrew Marvell is preferred for wit.
Through all the world from Chile to Cathay
260 The Re-search Empire still extends its sway.
Some genuine scholars—this, I grant, is true—
Still labour in the Old World and the New,
Refuse to dabble in that common sewer,
The pseudo-science now called *Literature*
Where harpies foul the feast, and dog eats dog,
And Footnote Fanny steers us through the fog.
On the far fringe, where this Pedantic Main
Slopes off into a vast erosion plain,
The Great South Land of the Antipodes,
270 The Yahoos have *their* universities,
And build with sticks and bones and flints obscene
Small models of the mighty Lit.-Machine;
And on this fringe's fringe there fusts unknown

257 bottòmless pit: bottòmless! what sort of language is this?
(A.A.P.)
The language of the divine Milton, son (*Paradise Lost*, VI, 864–6):
   headlong themselves they threw
  Down from the verge of Heav'n, Eternal wrath
  Burned after them to the bottomless pit.
Our author refers to Dr Leavis in his notorious attack on Milton,
*Revaluation*, pp. 42–61 and 26–8, an act of duncedom worthy of
your own; but he at least spared Pope and shall be saved at the
Last Day for this one just opinion in his critical Sodom. (A.P.)
260 Re-search: a New World pronunciation—not to be confused
with scholarship. (A.P.)

Arthur, Pretender to the Sable Throne;
And thus, from Philips down the line descends
From less to least and in a Phillips ends!

And now his due from the immortals here
He claims—as once Ithuriel with his spear
Gave Satan his full stature when he found
280    Him small and toad-like squatting on the ground,
Muttering some foulness in the ear of Eve,
Batrachian Arthur! Grant him this reprieve!
Touch him with satire; see him grow immense
In dullness, godlike in malevolence!
Left where he squats, in vain he croaks and froths.
If he expires, and unavenged—ye Goths,
While here they keep Augustan Holiday—'

'Now softly, friend! Compose yourself!' said Gay.
'No man may threaten or cajole the dead.
290    Over the gate these words you must have read:
"Here green with bays each ancient altar stands,

278ff.    Cf. *Paradise Lost*, IV, 810ff.:
        Him thus intent Ithuriel with his spear
        Touch'd lightly . . . up he starts
        Discovered and Surpris'd. As when a spark
        Lights on a heap of nitrous powder laid
        Fit for the Tun som Magasin to store . . .
        So started up in his own shape the Fiend. (A.P.)
285    Cf. Pope, *Epistle to Dr Arbuthnot* (character of Sporus):
        Or at the Ear of Eve, familiar Toad
        Half Froth, half Venom, spits himself abroad. (A.P.)
291–2    Pope, *An Essay on Criticism*, 181ff.:
        Still green with bays each ancient altar stands
        Above the reach of sacrilegious hands . . .
        O may some spark of your celestial fire
        The last, the meanest of your sons inspire,
        (That on weak wings, from far, pursues your flights
        Glows while he reads, but trembles as he writes)
        To teach vain wits a science little known,
        To admire superior sense, and doubt their own!
    I commend this passage to you, son! (A.P.)

Above the reach of sacrilegious hands."
Your case is stated, you may be at ease;
Now wait for judgment, sir, and hold your peace!'

The four immortals now to judgment came:
Two favoured, two opposed the hero's claim.
Said Gay: 'Why, let him have it; I declare,
One fool the more, 'tis neither here nor there!'
'Not so!' said Swift. 'So nugatory an ass
300    If mentioned has some weight, some power; whereas
Even the school-men to this truth confessed:
De minimis—dear Gay, you know the rest.'

'Yes,' said the doctor, 'I agree with Swift:
Such long confession calls for a short shrift.
And there's another reason: I oppose
Satire on persons, as our friend here knows.
When ridicule or censure make precise
The face of folly or the name of vice,
The world, which suffers fools as dogs their fleas,
310    Not general truth but simple scandal sees,
Blind to the love of strong and wholesome light,
Sees only the dark grounds of private spite.
Reflect, good friend, how often have you been
Accused of malice, pettiness and spleen
For this alone? Oblige this saucy Jack:
Straight he'll impute it to his lame attack,
Your wounded vanity—Best bid goodbye
With Hamlet's valediction to the spy.'

306ff.    as our friend here knows: cf. Epistle to Dr Arbuthnot, 100-2:
          Pope:    Still to one bishop Philips seems a Wit?
                   Still Sappho—
          Arbuthnot: Hold! for God's sake you'll offend.
                   No Names—be calm—learn Prudence of a Friend.
318      Hamlet, Act 3, sc. 4:
                   Thou wretched, rash, intruding fool, farewell!
                   I took thee for thy better.

'All that you say is true enough,' replied
320   The poet, 'yet I choose the other side.
No pest is harmless and where pests abound
Number, not size, lays waste the Muses' ground.
The war goes on, for critics never die;
Nor is it foolish to give fools the lie.
Not that my works or me, dear John, they hurt,
But that each sneer at art, all praise of dirt
Unanswered, helps corrupt the general mind;
And Beauty walks in vain once all are blind.
And do not tell me some though low, are good,
330   Unjustly punished or misunderstood.
Many a dunce I lashed with ridicule
I knew full well was not an utter fool:
Bentley was a sound scholar, I admit;
Cibber and Dennis had *some* claim to wit;
Theobald at least could keep account and spell,
And sometimes Namby-Pamby would write well.
All this, though true, is quite beside the point:
When Satire cries: "The time is out of joint!"
Then is no time to balance *ayes* and *noes*:
340   It is the side men fight on makes them foes.
Then he's a traitor who would make all smooth,
Pour oil, excuse and compromise with truth.
Lady Macbeth was a devoted wife,
And Torquemada led a saintly life—
Shall Satire, when the very stones cry out,
For this not let her dauntless trumpets shout?
She must speak out the more, denounce false shame,
Cry Murder! and give Savagery its name!
Nor ask me, John, as once you did in joke,
350   Why bother to attack where none provoke?

336   Mr Pope in a letter to his friend Cromwell confessed that I was
'capable of writing very nobly'. (A.P.)

When I see genius scanted, worth put down,
Though I'm not touched, the cause becomes my own.
Silence, of all accomplices, is best
And none are innocent where none protest.
No matter where the barb its victim finds,
The wound is mine, and yours and all mankind's.

But if in doubt, or friendship, still you say
The sport is cruel, labour thrown away
And think me wanting prudence, sense or heart,
360    Then I reply that Satire is an Art—
For here we touch great Nature's paradox,
A mystery my Dunciad unlocks:
As Heroes, creatures of eternal law,
Are born to brave the trials Heaven foresaw,
To slay the monsters and to save the state
And at their births the portents show them great;
As naked beauty, flattered by the brush,
Seems to put even nature to the blush.
And takes the painter's genius as her due,
370    Yet time soon shows that the reverse is true:
The mortal substance fades and falls apart,
But in its end and cause, the work of art,

358    The sport is cruel: cf. *Epistle to Dr Arbuthnot*, 83–4, 89–92:
        You think this cruel? Take it for a rule,
        No creature smarts as little as a Fool . . .
        Who shames a Scribler? break one cobweb thro',
        He spins the slight, self-pleasing thread anew;
        Destroy his Fib, or Sophistry; in vain,
        The Creature's at his dirty work again. (A.P.)
362    This refers to Mr Pope's *First* Dunciad. In a preface to the
edition of 1729: 'For whoever will consider the Unity of the
whole design, will be sensible, that the *Poem* was not made for
these Authors, but these Authors for the Poem.' An opinion
which time hath amply confirmed. (A.P.)

The creamy flank still breathes, the ripe breast glows,
When who the subject was none cares or knows.

So all bad critics, pedants, hacks, inane
And feeble scribblers ought not to complain
That, innocent of harm, they serve my need.
By Nature and by Providence decreed
For satire, let them live and ply their trade,
380    And own that for this purpose they were made!
So from the dung and dirt in which it grows
Evolves the flawless, breathless, living rose;
So pearls encrust themselves about a worm
And grubs enriched in amber cease to squirm;
So Arthur's prayer is granted!
                    But to live
Deathless in verse it is not mine to give.
Once he is dead an author's work is closed:
No syllable in what he once composed
May he obliterate or change or add;
390    And thus it stands, sir, with my Dunciad.
Yet still within my power it lies, I own,
To grant him the reversion of the throne:
The great-great-grandsire and the mighty son
Shall share A. Philips' footnote in Book One!
For though not very apposite, 'twill do;
And 'Thule' is enough to cover two;

383–5    Cf. *Epistle to Dr Arbuthnot*, 165–70 (again how aptly it fits my grandson!):
        Each Wight who reads not, and but scans and spells,
        Each Word-catcher that lives on syllables,
        E'en such small Critics some regard may claim
        Preserv'd in *Milton's* or in *Shakespear's* name.
        Pretty! in Amber to observe the forms
        Of hairs, or straws, or dirt, or grubs, or worms. (A.P.)
394    footnote: for that footnote, this footnote refers the reader to the footnote in Book I, 302 of the present Poem. This is the true joy of editorship! See Footnote Fanny! (A.P.)

Add editorial comment *quantum suff.*:
For him 'tis immortality enough!

You have your answer, Herald: bear it hence!
400    Let the great queen of Smut and Impudence
Transport her royal fledgling to the skies
At once—our pleasure is to see him rise!'

401    Transport: a word of peculiar significance in New Holland.
(A.P.)

## *End of Book III*

# BOOK IV

'Goddess, whose trust and sacred arms I bear,
Rejoice! the day is won; the coast is clear;
The wall is breached; the towers of Heaven down
And Arthur has his patent to the crown.
In every realm the great *nil obstat* runs;
Rich wines of Nonsense, sleeping in their tuns
Long ages, now shall flow in every street
And maudlin revel show his Fame complete.
Lo, I alone, inspired by your command,
10    From the vast deep have brought this fish to land;
By false submission and triumphant fraud
Seduced the sons of light to pledge their word;
My voice, your faithful slave, by devious wit,
Unworthy though I am, has compassed it;
Long exercised in wiles, on my return
Before your throne with conscious pride I burn.
But now, since for the nonce our cause is strong,
And Genius may be tricked, but not for long,
Be swift, lest on reflection they refuse;
20    Great Goddess, act! There is no time to lose;
For on my setting out the Fatal Four
Issued their edict and proclaimed their law:
It is their pleasure that our royal dunce
Assume his fathers' throne and rule at once.'
Thus far the Herald, as adust he stood
Before his mistress in vainglorious mood.

15    Cf. Pope's *Odyssey*, I, 2:
        The man for wisdom's various arts renown'd,
        Long exercised in woes, O Muse! resound ... (A.P.)

45

A venal trollop, tumbled in the hay,
Could not be more perfidiously gay.
But, wrapped in mists that choke the Stygian stye,
30    The awful shade at first makes no reply.
Then on her slave, as on an errant spouse,
She looks and glooms and bends her ireful brows:
'What, sirrah, counsel you in things divine
And dare to interpose in *my* design?
Infected by the air of Heaven, I see
You venture to give orders, then, to Me;
Me, sir, a goddess, to my very face
Told to bestir myself and mend my pace?
You have fulfilled your errand; this I own,
40    But curb your insolence before my throne!
Let Heaven issue edicts as it please:
Its writ runs not below nor its decrees;
Their cause is lost; the times are in my hand;
'Tis mine and mine alone now to command.
Arthur shall rise, but in my own good time,
And, ere he soars to that inane sublime,
As fits a hero of the ancient breed,
His Funeral Games on earth I have decreed.'

'Pardon, great Queen, my error I admit.
50    Pardon, if still in judgment or in wit
I should appear in deed or thought or word
To deviate from the true, the pure Absurd.'
Replies the unhappy brute and shakes his head:
'But funerals are surely for the dead!
My mind miscarries and my heart misgives:
How can this be while noble Arthur lives?'

32    her ireful brows: cf. Marlowe, *Dr Faustus*, Act 5, sc. 2, 154–5:
        and see where God
        Stretcheth out his arm and bends his ireful brows. (A.P.)

The Goddess smiles and heaves her ample breast
To mirth, for Dullness dearly loves a jest.
The vast bulk rumbles as her head she nods:
60 'Hear, witling, hear the laughter of the gods
And learn at last whate'er I do is right:
Nonsense it is! In Nonsense I delight.
I grant that Arthur lives, but even so,
What if he does, child? Who on earth would know?
Remember Partridge who foretold the date
Of royal demise and high events of state,
Whom Bickerstaff (for Bickerstaff, read Swift)
Foretold would die and promised a short shrift;
The day came on; though Partridge might protest,
70 The Devil had his soul, the wits their jest.
It was not in his choice to live or die.
If Swift could compass this, so, sir, may I.
Nor is it yours, friend, to dispute the case:
A cat may have less lives than Arthur has.

Besides, these Funeral Games I have designed
Are not for him, but for the human mind,

58    loves a jest: cf. *Dunciad*, II, 33–4:
           Glory and gain, th' industrious tribe provoke
           And gentle Dullness ever loves a joke.
61    I do is right: An echo, son, from the poem you traduced; cf.
      Pope, *An Essay on Man*, IV, 393–4:
           For Wit's false mirror held up Nature's light
           Shew'd erring Pride, WHATEVER is, IS RIGHT . . . (A.P.)
65    Partridge: what was this, grandad? (A.A.P.)
      An unhappy cobbler called Partridge, son, an astrologer whose
      own death was foretold by Dr Swift in the name of Isaac
      Bickerstaff and then confirmed. When Partridge protested, the
      wits conspired to prove him really dead. Like you, he presumed
      to meddle with Fate. (A.P.)
70    the wits their jest: so Dryden, *Absolom and Achitophel*, II, 561–2:
           Beggared by fools, whom still he found too late,
           He had his jest, and they had his estate. (A.P.)

The death of wit, the last eclipse of taste
And gales of nonsense howling through the waste.
As those at young Patroclus' pyre decreed,
80    Though to placate his restless shade indeed,
Were less to celebrate the hapless boy
Than Hector's death that spelled the doom of Troy,
So, in my darker purpose, I propose
More things than you, sir, or than Arthur knows:
He, though he errs, in that old world believes
Where genius by right its due receives,
Where worth in its tradition trusts and rests
And Criticism to its place attests;
Nor is he always brash or led astray:
90    At times some Austral writers own his sway;
And if he fell, in honest faith he erred;
Now a new age brings in the real Absurd,
Where critics in their pride themselves replace
Their cause and consequence, the scribbling race.
Their cause is now themselves, the consequence
The topsy-turveydom of wit and sense.
These are my darling sons; until they rule
Let Arthur squat upon his royal stool.
The Merovingians doddering to their fall
100   Ruled through the palace mayors, if at all;
But when the time was ripe, they fell from view.
Some mighty Charles of Dullness now is due,

79    Patroclus: cf. Pope's *Iliad*, Book XXIII. (A.P.)
83    my darker purpose: so *King Lear*, Act 1, sc. 1, 38–9:
       Meanwhile we shall express our darker purpose.
       Give me the map there. (A.P.)
102   Mighty Charles: the father of Carolus Magnus, then mayor of
the palace, deposed his royal master and divided the empire of
the Franks between his sons. Our author intends a like fate for
you and our time. (A.P.)

And him my provident design proclaims
By the dire pretext of these Funeral Games.

But dream not of such games as heroes played
When on the pyre Achilles' love was laid;
Nor those a pious son ordained before
His father's tomb on the Sicilian shore;
Not even such wanton frolics in the mud
110   As graced the dunces at the gates of Lud;
Nor such as Arthur's chosen Seat has made
The sites where Austral football still is played
Where in the wintry season, full of beer
Poet and peasant, churl and sage appear
Shriek with unreason, stultify the soul,
To see a pig-skin booted through the goal.
Games, I would have you know sir, nowadays
Renounce that joyous strife to win the bays
Which in more spacious times, a doubtful dream,
120   Still fired the crowd and fortified the team.
The Science of Prediction now moves in
To fore-ordain and blight their will to win,
And Mathematics claims, by dubious art,
To prophesy the end before they start.
As critics now annex the poet's crown,

107   pious son: Aeneas (A.P.)
110   the gates of Lud: *Dunciad*, II, 359–60:
      Thro' Lud's fam'd gates, along the well-known Fleet,
      Rolls the black troop, and over shades the street.
111   Arthur's . . . Seat: surely an error of our author here? (A.P.)
    Not the famous hill in Edinburgh, grandad, but an eminence not
    far from Melbourne, here used generally of my native city.
    (A.A.P.)
114   Poet and Peasant: football, son? Football is a game for idle
    apprentices and the city rabble. (A.P.)
    Not in this age, grandad. Next to the horse it is the great re-
    ligion of the Southern Yahoos. The poets of my city are its
    particular devotees. (A.A.P.)

Theory of Games is up and Sport is down.
Now every player makes his move in fear
With statisticians muttering in his ear;
Computers oust onlookers from the field
130   Advising when to strike and when to yield;
Hockey or Prisoners' Base, Tip-cat or Chess
Run to foregone conclusions more or less;
And even War, the game of games, must halt
When umpires with their slide-rules utter: Fault!
Though stubborn hearts, contending in the dust,
On native wit and inborn vigour trust,
And little max-mins still the gods defy

126–40   Theory of Games . . . max-mins . . . decimals: all this is Greek
to me, son. (A.P.)
Theory of Games, grandad, is a new invention of the Academy
of Lagado. To give you a notion of the ingeniously barbarous
jargon of this science, let me quote you a passage from two of its
chief wizards (Tucker and Kuhn, *The Theory of Games*). A and
B are to be supposed playing a game against each other: 'So to
maximize his assumed gains on the assumption that B knows his
strategy and will counter all moves to make A's gains as small as
possible, A is led to seek a maximum of minima (abbreviate to
*max-min*). The . . . aim of B is to choose a course of action that
will hold to a minimum of maxima the greatest loss A may inflict.
Thus B's goal is a minimum of maxima (abbreviated to *min-max*).
The clear fact that A cannot establish a floor under his possible
gains that is higher than the ceiling B succeeds in placing over his
possible losses is expressed by the formula:
A's gain-floor = max-min ⩽ min-max
= B's loss ceiling.' This should make it all clear to
you, grandad. (A.A.P.)
Still Greek to me, son. Do the new critics understand all this?
(A.P.)
No, grandad, but many of them use computers for their black art.
(A.A.P.)
137   'max-mins': Our author here ingeniously echoes Dryden,
*Mac Flecknoe*, 76–8:
Where unfledg'd Actors learn to laugh and cry,
Where infant Punks their tender voices try,
And little *Maximins* the Gods defy. (A.P.)

Armed with the mystic decimals of *Pi*,
They strive in vain: such Funeral Games, indeed
140    Befit my critics of the latest breed.
My grand design thus far revealed, although
Things still suppressed in night seek not to know,
Now, Herald, I have further tasks for you;
So stir your stumps, for there is much to do.
Before dawn reddens in the sullen sky
To every fane of learning you must fly;
By each bad critic's pillow stand and don
The shape his dream of fame most dotes upon:
A variorum text; a printer's fee;
150    A grant, a knighthood or a rare Litt.D.
Some genius smirched and scanted of his fame,
Or drowned in sources, which is much the same;
Or, what the academic soul prefers,
Some theory, so befuddled and perverse,
As makes all criticism seem a farce
And wins a chair to dignify his arse.
Soon as he wakes and spies the tempting bait,
My contest put before him and the date;
Bid each devise some mad machine, designed
160    To warp the judgment and pervert the mind,
Some engine foul in smell that blurts and spits
To muddle verse and addle readers' wits
And ride it belching through the etherial blue,
Uttering the criticaster's View-Halloo!
Last in each ear the flattering message hiss:
The prize is in his grasp: he cannot miss.
Within an hour, for sure, we shall descry
Their inky legions tumbling from the sky.'

142    suppressed in night: so Milton, *Paradise Lost*, VII, 122-4:
                nor let thine own inventions hope
        Things not reveald, which th' invisible King,
        Onely Omniscient, hath supprest in Night. (A.P.)

The Herald bowed and vanished with a bang,
170   A sulphurous stench and unmelodious twang.
While Dullness settling hugely for her nap,
Drowses in confidence to spring her trap;
And not in vain: the trap is duly sprung.
She wakes to hear her sooty hounds give tongue
And, from the darkening air, with hideous sound,
A pride of critics plummet and rebound.
Smug in their hopes and livid with their spleen,
They cut their engines and salute their queen,
Who takes their graceless plaudits as her due
180   And grins complacent on the grisly crew.
The grisly crew, as smug, return her grin
To hear the Queen of Nonsense thus begin:

'Welcome, dear sons, of all my sons the best!
And proud must be the heart within this breast,
Goggled and helmeted to see you stand
Like locusts swarming to devour the land.
Your loyal service first of all I praise,
The Lyre unstrung, the sere and wilted Bays,
Pedantry loosed on its unbridled course,
190   The Sacred Spring polluted at its source,
Critical smog infecting every breeze
While strangling theories choke the noblest trees.
These are your works! Your triumphs I confess
And with maternal fondness praise and bless.

170   twang: cf. John Aubrey, *Miscellanies*: 'Anno 1670, not far from
Cirencester, was an apparition: being demanded whether a good
spirit or bad? returned no answer, but disappeared with a curious
perfume and a most melodious twang.'
This effect of dullness has been applied by the poet Byron to
Southey's reading of his works: *The Vision of Judgment*, stanza 3:
    But at the fourth, the whole spiritual show
    Had vanished with variety of scents,
    Ambrosial and sulphureous, as they sprang,
    Like lightning, off from his 'melodious twang'. (A.P.)

But more than these conclusive victories
I praise your stratagem to hold the peace,
Secure me henceforth empire of the pen
And drive out wit if it should come again.
Your constant vigilance a means supplies
200    To stultify young poets as they rise;
By education damp and render tame
Fresh genius; dim and quench the sacred flame;
Taught not to venture past the common reach
By those who cannot do and therefore teach,
And, once emasculated by your rules,
To warble in Creative Writing Schools.
Let Malcolm Cowley thunder as he will:
Who now reads Cowley? I am Dullness still!
Sheer bulk and weight of comment now ensure
210    By slow degrees the death of literature;
A book, no sooner born, is buried straight
By fifty more of critical debate
And, rising year by year, the monstrous flood
Deposits new layers of explicatory mud.
Choked in the sludge, all authors, good or bad
Soon lose what meaning they might once have had.
Few readers now remember that the right

204    therefore teach: what is this, son? (A.P.)
A scandalous attack on our whole profession by a modern wit,
now happily extinct, grandad. See Bernard Shaw, *Maxims for
Revolutionaries*: 'He who can, does. He who cannot, teaches.'
(A.A.P.)
206    Creative Writing Schools: what again is this? (A.P.)
A modern device, grandad, to get young Samsons blind to the
critic's mill. (A.A.P.)
207    Malcolm Cowley: ? (A.P.)
A great last-ditcher of our time, grandad: 'all these novelists
show the influence of the newer criticism. All the novelists have
a double audience in mind: first there is the broader public they
would like to reach without really trying, and second there are
the critics they must be sure to please.' (Malcolm Cowley, *The
Literary Situation*) (A.A.P.)

True end of verse was wisdom and delight,
But taught by you, my sons, conceive it is
220   The endless nausea of analysis.
The Wingèd Horse, once trampling in his pride,
See now securely to his manger tied;
Struggle he may: be sure the die is cast:
His own by-products bury him at last,
Till in the dung of this Augean stall
Most readers cannot find a horse at all.
And to this end—my sovereign plot confessed—
The sons of Light contribute with the rest.
In this vast scribbledom by fate immersed
230   The best of critics wallow like the worst:
Provided they will write and write and write,
They serve the cause of Chaos and of Night.
Think not by this I mean to scant your worth
Yours is the prize. You brought this plague to birth;
For you and you alone, these Funeral Games,
Sons of my womb, a mother's care proclaims.
Each, as perverted genius prompts, has been
Inventor of some critical machine
Designed to make true genius seem perverse
240   And sow confusion in the Art of Verse.
These engines now before my eyes display:
Who proves the most absurd shall win the day.
Come, prime and crank the monsters for the start!
And lest you should lack victims for your art,
With prescient and preventive care, I have
Summoned a batch of authors from the grave,
Picked for their fame, the noblest and the best
Of all whom in my heart I most detest.
Although but simulacra formed from air

218-19   the right, true end: cf. Donne, *Elegies*, XVIII:
        Whoever loves, if he do not propose
        The right true end of love, he's one that goes
        To sea for nothing but to make him sick.

250    These let your rabid malice maul and tear.
Behold this tomb where mighty Arthur lies;
There let them bleed, a welcome sacrifice!'
She ceased. While pandemoniums of applause
Roaring exhausts, wild shrieks and gnashing jaws
Shattered the air, by Endor's arts she drew
Before their eyes a pale and ghastly crew,
Chained, starved and bullied, ragged to a man;
Chaucer in tatters leads the trembling van;
Milton by slashing Bentley maimed and scarred;
260    Shakespeare in Bacon's feathers, pitched and tarred;
Pope spattered from the filthy Grub-street stye;
Marlowe, a critic's dagger through his eye;
Clare starving from his dunghill led like Job,
And Smart from Bedlam pelted by the mob;
Chatterton mocked on his untimely bed;
Dryden with Blackmore's piss-pot on his head;
Keats, a forlorn Sebastian, skewered through
With shafts of Blackwood's venomous review;

251    this tomb: but grandad—! (A.A.P.)
Tut! remember Partridge, son! (A.P.)
252    sacrifice: our author here imitates the sacrifice of Trojan victims
at the pyre of Patroclus. Pope's *Iliad*, XXIII, 27–32:
> Behold! *Achilles'* Promise is compleat;
> The bloody *Hector* stretch'd before thy feet.
> Lo! to the Dogs his Carcass *I* resign;
> And twelve sad Victims at the *Trojan* line
> Sacred to Vengeance, instant shall expire;
> Their lives effus'd around thy Funeral Pyre. (A.P.)
255    Endor's arts: cf. 1 Samuel 28: 1–25; our author here perhaps
refers to a similar event in Mr Pope's *Dunciad*, II, 35–6:
> A Poet's form she plac'd before their eyes
> And bade the nimblest racer seize the prize. (A.P.)
266    Blackmore's piss-pot: I never heard of this. (A.A.P.)
Sir Richard Blackmore's graceless attack on this great poet in his
days of misery, son. *Prince Arthur*, Book VI:
> Laurus amidst the Meagre Crowd appear'd,
> An Old, Revolted, Unbelieving Bard,
> Who Throng'd and Shov'd and Press'd and would be heard.

I spare you the rest of this filth. (A.P.)

All these and many more the goddess there
270 Exposed, exclaiming: 'Smite and do not spare!
The vengeance by the Critic Race of old
Exacted, here, my sons, you may behold.
Lay on! Let their example boost your fires
And prove you butchers worthy of your sires!'
The pack runs howling on its destined prey;
The hapless victims shrink and cower away;
But, as they slaver, grim in tooth and claw,
The genial ghost of Shakespeare steps before,
Smiling, serene, he checks them unafraid;
280 Then turns to utter words of cheer and aid:

'Be of good heart, my friends! We know the worst
These dogs can do, for they are not the first.
The wolf's black jaw and the dull ass's hoof
We need not dread; Time gives us ample proof.
Dullness is its own remedy and curse,
Digs its own grave and decks its own poor hearse.
These are but shades of fear and men of straw;
A few short years they may impose their law,
But the next age shall raise us from the dead,
290 Keep green our fame and leave their screeds unread
And where their Babel moulders, smile to see
Burgeon the fruitful vine and blossoming tree.'

Scarce had he spoken: rumbling in her wrath,
The outraged Queen bestrides the poet's path;

283     the wolf's jaw: Ben Jonson, surely! He makes Shakespeare a
plagiarist, grandad! (A.A.P.)
Like the early Christians, son, the poets have all things in common
and laugh at source-hunters. (A.P.)
291     where their Babel moulders: so Pope on Timon's villa in *Epistle
to the Earl of Burlington*, 173–6:
> Another age shall see the golden Ear
> Imbrown the Slope, and nod on the Parterre,
> Deep Harvests bury all his pride has plann'd,
> And laughing Ceres re-assume the land. (A.P.)

With fury first her talons wrench and tear;
Next see the wretched bard snatched high in air;
His rib-bones crack, as in a bear-like hug,
She strains him to her bosom's fog and fug;
Last, hurled to earth, she views him crushed and dead
300    And bids her critics tear him shred from shred.
The critics hesitate: 'Alas, great Queen,
How tear him more than he's already been?
Dissolved in sources, emendated, glossed,
Ripped leaf from leaf and like a salad tossed,
By turns, now mutilated, now restored,
Volumes of commentary on each word,
By actors mangled, travestied and cut,
By Bishop Wordsworth bowdlerized from smut,
Riddled and soused in Theory's witches' brew,
310    With, Shakespeare, Lady, what is left to do?'
But while they waver, sadly at a stay,
By unseen hands the corpse is rapt away
And, the next instant, to abate their fears,
Smiling the poet stands among his peers.
The Goddess swells and roars with helpless rage
316    And bids the combatants at once engage.

312    rapt away: What rubbish is this, grandad? (A.A.P.)
Our author intends here, son, a parallel with the saving of Hector's
body from the vengeance of Achilles. Pope's *Iliad*, XXIII, 11:
    'But Heavier Fates on *Hector*'s Corse attend,
    Sav'd from the Flames for hungry Dogs to rend.'
    So spoke he, threat'ning: But the Gods made vain
    His threat, and guard inviolate the Slain:
    Celestial *Venus* hover'd o'er his Head,
    And roseate Unguents, heav'nly Fragrance shed:
    She watch'd him all the Night, and all the Day,
    And drove the Bloodhounds from their destin'd Prey.

## End of Book IV

# BOOK V

Now Muse assist me, aptly to describe
Mechanic contests of the Critic tribe;
Choose but condign exemplars for my song,
Lest, like themselves, I explicate too long;
Let me shed light on things both dark and dense
Yet never move them into common sense.

First of the few for whom the Muse finds space,
See Wilson Knight advance and take his place.
A Double Boiler fixed on fiery wheels,
10   Hisses hysteric or ecstatic squeals;
He takes a play, *The Tempest*, from his poke,
Kisses the boards and drops it in the smoke.
The smoke redoubles and the cauldron roars;
At length he turns a cock and out there pours
The play—Ah, no! it cannot be the play
To myth and symbolism boiled away;
Where are the plot, the actors and the stage?
These are irrelevant, explains the sage;
Damn action and discourse: The play's no more

1–6   Our author here recalls the sublime invocation of Milton's Muse,
        *Paradise Lost*, Book VII, 1–39. (A.P.)
9     fiery wheels: why fiery wheels, son? (A.P.)
        A reference, grandad, to a work by this author, *The Wheel of
        Fire*. (A.A.P.)
16, 20   myth and symbolism . . . extended metaphor: '*The Tempest* will
        be found peculiarly poor in metaphor. There is less need for it in
        that the play itself is a metaphor.' (Wilson Knight, *The Crown of
        Life*) (A.A.P.)
19     Damn action: see Pope, *Epistle to Augustus*, 314–15:
                The Play stands still; damn action and discourse,
                Back fly the scenes, and enter foot and horse . . .

20   Than drifts of an extended metaphor
Did simple Shakespeare think: 'The play's the thing'?
What Shakespeare thought is hustled from the ring.
He's shouted down: 'Fallacious by intent';
Critics repudiate what the author meant.
Is *Lear* the story of a King? Ah, no,
A tract on clothing and what lurks below.
Well, but the audience came to see men act
And not to hear a philosophic tract?
Wrong once again, my friend: we won't admit
30   That many-headed monster of the pit,
Who think *The Tempest* tells a tale perhaps
And not a long-drawn metaphor, poor chaps;
In three short hours how could *they* hope to judge
What takes a critic twenty years of drudge?
But who would write a play with this in view?
That only proves that Shakespeare scorned them too.
A sovereign critic is a mighty god;
Author and audience vanish at his nod;
He takes the poet's place, re-weaves the spell,
40   And is its only audience as well.

Scarce had the Goddess viewed this weird machine,
When envious Leavis thrusts himself between;

23   Fallacious by intent: see Wimsatt and Beardsley, *The Intentional Fallacy* (1946). Did they really hold this monstrous opinion, son? (A.P.)
No, grandad, to give them their due. But they launched the idea. (A.A.P.)
28   a tract on clothing: see Robert Heilman, 'Poor Naked Wretches and Proud Array', in *This Great Stage* (1948).
30   many-headed monster: see Pope, *Epistle to Augustus*, 304–5:
        There still remains to mortify a Wit,
        The many-headed Monster of the Pit. (A.P)
On the same side, but very cautious, see Cleanth Brooks: *The Formalist Critic*. (A.A.P.)
39   a mighty god: Marlowe, *Dr Faustus*, sc. 1, 61:
        A sound magician is a demi-god . . .

Cries: 'What, infringe my patent, thievish swine!
The "extended metaphor" conceit is mine,
Mine the "dramatic poem" device, I say,
By which I demonstrate a play's no play.
Ignore him, Goddess; turn those eyes divine
From Wilson's shandrydan and gaze on mine!
In shining nickel and unblushing brass
50   Streamlined to make a genius seem an ass,
Reverse the judgment of the centuries,
Make and unmake Tradition as I please,
Exalt the lowly and put down the great.
Observe now while I prestidigitate!'

So saying he thrusts great Fielding in his pot
And in beside him tumbles Walter Scott;
Pours in some gallons of high-octane spleen;
Fiddles and draws a belch from the machine;
Hey Presto! From a trap-door there escape
60   A hunch-back pigmy and a crippled ape.
'Behold my triumph, Queen!', the critic cries,
'My metamorphoses confound all eyes.
Can this be Fielding whom they knew immense
For wit and charity and common sense?
No, a mere tyro—take a second view—
From whom Jane Austen learned a trick or two.

52ff.   See the cavalier treatment of Scott and Fielding in F. R. Leavis,
*The Great Tradition* (1948).

55–70   See *The Great Tradition*: 'Fielding . . . hasn't the classical impor-
tance we are . . . invited to credit him with. He is important . . .
because he leads to Jane Austen to appreciate whose distinction is
to feel that life isn't long enough to permit of one's giving much
time to Fielding.'
'Scott was primarily a kind of inspired folk-lorist, qualified to
have done in fiction something analogous to the ballad-opera . . .
not having the creative writer's interest in literature, he made no
serious attempt to work out his own form and break away from
the bad tradition of the eighteenth century romance.'
Who made this mad Jack a judge in Israel, son? (A.P.)
Self-made! (A.A.P.)

Can this be Scott, then, whose magician's quill
Delighted Europe and delights it still?
Not so! Look once again: my art unveils
70    A dabbler in romance and old wives' tales.'
At this the Goddess smiles and nods her head:
'Who then, dear son, would you exalt instead?'
'Observe, great Matriarch,' her son replies,
'This mannikin, the sport of wasps and flies,
Peevish and arrogant, he vents a flood
Of words which he calls "thinking with the blood";
With generous Fielding, or with noble Scott
Compared, he shrinks and dwindles and is not.
And now—watch carefully—in my machine
80    I place him; add some drops of wintergreen,
A pinch of scrutiny, a touch of gall,
And D. H. Lawrence towers over all.'

There was a moment's silence then a howl
Of jealous rivals: 'Out! A Foul! A Foul!'
The Goddess pursed her lips and then she smiled:
'Such stratagems would not deceive a child,
Remove these baubles; let the Games proceed
And bring me critics of a sterner breed.'

Next from the ranks comes clucking T. R. Henn
90    Attended by a train of faceless men;
And at his side, in female garb, there move
Caroline Spurgeon, Rosamunda Tuve;
Blest pair of Sirens, dredges of Heav'n's joy,
His mother and his aunt, their charms employ
To prove, though art is long and life is short

74    wasps and flies: what is this, grandad? (A.A.P.)
       Our author, son, is thinking of Gulliver's adventure with the
       wasps in Brobdignag. (A.P.)
93    Sirens: see Milton, *At a Solemn Musick*, 1-2:
       Blest pair of *Sirens*, pledges of Heav'n's joy
       Sphear-born harmonious Sisters, Voice and Vers. (A.P.)

That Drake and Shakespeare shared a favourite sport
And demonstrate *ad nauseam* the way
By Tudor rhetoric to build a play.
(Read them, alas, discover to your cost:
100    The proof's irrelevant; the play is lost.)
These chicks, for mighty Henn, who stalks between,
Push forward an ingenious machine
As full of pigeon-holes, as bare of birds
As those the Record Office stuffs with words.
Great Henn dismisses them, affects to nod,
Selects a poet and assumes the god.

'You call on us, great Queen, and not in vain.
Ours is a subtler, more insidious strain.
Ours not to denigrate, pervert, deny
110    Or puff inferior scribblers to the sky;
Patient and meek, we seize on honest worth
And, like the meek, inheriting the earth,

96–7    sport . . . *ad nauseam*: a fine example of two opposite kinds of
irrelevance in the same school of criticism, grandad. Caroline
Spurgeon, *Shakespeare's Imagery and What it Tells Us*: 'of all the
exercises Shakespeare mentions—tennis, football, bowls, fencing,
tilting, wrestling—there can be no doubt that bowls was the one
he himself played and loved the best. He has nineteen images
from bowls beside other references.' (A.A.P.)
He has more references to fornication, son; does this prove him
a fornicator? (A.P.)
Rosamund Tuve, *Elizabethan Imagery*. (A.A.P.)
No quotation, son? (A.P.)
Not from *me*, grandad. (A.A.P.)
105–6    'affects to nod': so Alexander the Great in Dryden's *Alexander's
Feast or the Power of Musique*:
          A present Deity, they shout around
          A present Deity, the vaulted Roofs resound.
               With ravish't ears
               The monarch hears,
               Assumes the God,
               Affects to nod,
          And seems to shake the Spheares. (A.P.)

We take them over, make them ours perforce,
Trace every image to its remotest source,
Load it with analogues, gild, trick and frost;
Meaning runs into meaning and is lost;
We read between the lines and read again
Between those lines inserted by our pen;
Add statues, pictures, junk and bric-à-brac
120  Until the poem's fabric starts to crack
And trick the guileless reader to believe
We still have something further up our sleeve,
Without which, though now driven to the wall,
He cannot understand the poem at all.
Faced with this parasitic mould indeed,
Readers, intimidated, cease to read.
The pleasure of discovery denied,
No corner left where mystery may hide;
And even the simplest poem seems obscure
130  When every root's confused with its manure.
Come, here's a poem of William Butler Yeats:
This simple thing my genius recreates;
Processed and pulped in my machine, it grows
To fifty pages of inspissate prose.
It is my boast, dear Mother, by this trick
To have found him marble and have left him brick.
Now watch me, Goddess, to confirm my claim,
Take Shakespeare next and treat him much the same.'

Thus far he spoke, when rose a general shout:
140  In rushed a psychoanalytic rout;

131  Yeats: what is this about, son? (A.P.)
    T. R. Henn, *The Lonely Tower: Studies in the poetry of W. B. Yeats,*
    grandad, a signal example of the Infinite Regress School of Ex-
    plication. (A.A.P.)
136  have left him brick: so Suetonius of Augustus: 'Urbem . .
    excoluit adeo, ut iure sit gloriatus marmoream se relinquere, quam
    latericam accepisset.' (A.P.)

Machines they pushed of every shape and size
That mind or myth or madness could devise.
Before them, rattling Shakespeare's honoured bones,
Lumbers the burly form of Ernest Jones:
'Have done with literary chit and chat!
What, Bullough come again? No more of that!
Ur-Hamlets? Fudge! Old Saxo? Tush and Pish!
Castration Fantasies, the dark Death Wish,
Oedipus Complex, narcissistic blocks:
150   This Key and this alone his heart unlocks.
As for esthetic theories, save your breath!
Topsoil at most; the pay-dirt lurks beneath;
Learn that all literature is fantasy,
All art, Neurosis which you cannot see.
The endless carping of the Leavisites,
Chatter of Cleanth Brooks and L. C. Knights,
What underlies their cultural debate?
A secret wish their fathers to castrate!
And as for Henn's Compulsive Ritual,
160   Anal Fixation will explain it all.
See, Goddess, see: their fictions I destroy!

141-2   So Dryden, *Absalom and Achitophel*:
        Gods they had tried of every shape and size
        That God-smiths could produce or Priests devise. (A.P.)

146   Bullough come again?: our author here, grandad, refers to the
learned Geoffrey Bullough's *Narrative and Dramatic Sources of
Shakespeare*, a work in innumerable volumes and millions of
words. There is also a hint at this critic's place among his peers
in the echo from Byron, *The Vision of Judgment*, stanza 93:
        The Monarch, mute till then, exclaimed: 'What! What!
        *Pye* come again? No more—no more of that!'

150   Key: Wordsworth, *Miscellaneous Sonnets*, part II, i:
        with this Key
        Shakespeare unlocked his heart.

153-4   So Pope, *An Essay on Man*, I, 289-90:
        All Nature is but Art unknown to thee;
        All Chance direction which thou canst not see . . . (A.P.)

Come, where is Herbert Read, my whipping boy?
Wheel me that Viennese contraption there!
Now fetch me *Hamlet*—handle him with care—
Now press this button and let in your clutch:
The play which Shakespeare wrote in Double Dutch,
Which lay dissolved in endless Wilson Knight,
Behold! Let Freud appear and all is light!
Was Hamlet mad or indecisive? Come,
170    He simply longed to go to bed with Mum;
And so did Shakespeare: "to avoid worse rape",
He found this mechanism of escape.
Good-night, Sweet Prince; to dream, perchance to skid
Between your Super-ego and your Id!'

He ceased. While hate and hubbub flew around,
The critics gnashed their teeth; the Goddess frowned:
'Your scheme, as far as I can make it out,
Destroys my foes, and yet I stand in doubt.
I read your heart, sir; in that heart I see
180    A sly, libidinous design on *me*,
Your mother and your queen. That purpose is
To deal with me as Oedipus with his.
Presumptuous slave!' . . . A shriek arrests her tongue
And furious Maud comes striding through the throng:

162    Herbert Read: our author refers to an essay, 'Psycho-analysis
and Criticism', in this critic's *Reason and Romanticism* (1926).
(A.A.P.)
167    dissolved . . . in Knight: so Pope, *Epitaph Intended for Sir Isaac
Newton*:
        Nature, and Nature's Laws lay hid in Night.
        God said, *Let Newton* be! and all was *Light*.
171    worse rape: so Milton, *Paradise Lost*, I, 503–5:
        Witness the streets of Sodom, and that night
        In Gibeah, when the hospitable door
        Expos'd a Matron to avoid worse rape.
183–202    What is all this about, son? (A.P.)
It would take too long to explain, grandad. See Maud Bodkin's
curious essay, 'A Study of the "Ancient Mariner" and of the Re-
birth Archetype', *Archetypal Patterns in Poetry* (1934). (A.A.P.)

'Jung, Mother Jung's the name to conjure with!
Poems are simply archetypal myth;
Poets, blind mouths through which Old Chaos streams;
And Racial Memory dictates their dreams.
A woman to a woman, hear my cry:
190    As I am Bodkin, let this traitor die!'
She spoke and with her weapon pierced him through.
While consternation seized the manly crew,
The Amazon bestrides the corpse of Jones,
Splits up his hide and extricates the bones,
Smears them with unguent from a shaman's pot
And Jones becomes the thing that he was not.
Reclothed with flesh, though stricken well in years,
An Ancient Mariner he now appears;
An albatross about his neck is hung;
200    He sings a Vedic hymn and calls on Jung!
The Goddess smiles: the critics all applaud:
'Behold a Rebirth Archetype!' cries Maud.
A New Medea, she towers to the skies
And stands in expectation of the prize.

Just then a form of more plebeian mould
Cries in stentorian tones: 'Hold, Goddess, hold!
Beware the muddles of the bourgeoisie;
For genuine muddle listen first to me!'
And, a left-legged Jacob, squat and wide,

200    Vedic hymn: Bodkin, ibid.: 'Dr. Jung cites from the Vedic
Hymns lines where prayers or ritual fire-boring, are said to lead
forth, or release the flowing streams of Rita.' (A.A.P.)
Not very nice is it, son? (A.P.)
Not very relevant to anything, either! (A.A.P.)
209    left-legged Jacob: so Pope, *Dunciad*, II, 65–8, describes the book-
seller Lintot:
          So lab'ring on, with shoulders, hands and head,
          Wide as a windmill, all his fingers spread,
          With arms expanded, Bernard rows his state
          And left-legg'd Jacob seems to emulate.
Our author's reference here is less to the Patriarch's wrestle with
the angel, than to a political stance. (A.A.P.)

210 With David Daiches trotting by his side,
Christopher Caudwell issues from the ranks,
Backed by a threatening brace of Soviet tanks.
The tanks advance; the critics all give ground;
He views the various machines around:
'This bourgeois junk, these antiquated arks!
No, Goddess, learn from Lenin and from Marx!
These are but children, squabbling at their play;
In Muscovy we take a shorter way:
The trial, the concentration camp, the knout,
220 Decide what literature is all about.
(Think of Akhmatova and Pasternak—)
Something your western bourgeois cultures lack
Are these two critical machines behind
The readiest way to halt the march of mind.'

'Son,' cries the Queen, 'although I sympathize,
This would not do yet in democracies.
There for the nonce, a better way to win
Is the slow rot of judgment from within;
Perhaps in any case a better way;
230 For violence breeds martyrs, so they say;
The hangman and the headsman and the stake
Are apt to raise rebellion in their wake,
Whereas a mind corrupted by degrees
Slides into Vacancy and calls it Peace.'
'Well, from your contest, then I must withdraw,
Dear Mother, till the reign of martial law;
Besides, a news-flash from the Chosen Land
Tells me that poets have got out of hand;
My thugs are needed there; I must return
240 And heads will roll while ivory towers burn.
Meantime, with blessings on this company,
I leave you Daiches here; no Marxist he,

234 calls it Peace: so Tacitus, *Agricola*: 'Ubi solitudinem faciunt,
pacem appellant.'

But fit to sow confusion: his machine
Tests art by mirrors. Should the social scene
Show a left-wing reflection of a tale,
Though dull, it passes, but if not, must fail.
Spenser and Malory to him are dross
And Rabelais and Sidney a dead loss.
Farewell, *pro tem.*; your Godhead I salute,
250    This *Lumpenprofessoriat* to boot.'
He raised his arm aloft and clenched his fist,
(Warning to every deviationist).
The tanks roll off; the critics roll an eye
And even David Daiches heaves a sigh.
A pause ensues: the Games are at a stand
Until the Goddess lifts her royal hand:
'Bring on the pachyderms of *Much Ado*,
My Formal Critics marching two and two!'
And from their verbal jungle to the bar,
260    Chanting a solemn dead march, from afar
Majestic in their pace and bearing, come
The Mastodons of Meaning, all and some.
Spokesmen and leaders of this lumbering crowd,
See Cleanth Brooks and Empson trumpet loud,
Wreathing the lithe proboscis in duet,

244    tests art by mirrors: David Daiches, 'Fiction and Civilisation', in
*The Novel and the Modern World*: 'What then is a great work of
art? . . . we shall probably find that the greatest works are those
which, while fulfilling all the formal requirements, most ade-
quately reflect the civilisation of which they are a product . . .
There will always be aspects of human character and emotion as
an illumination of which the decadent bourgeoisie, the struggling
proletariat, the atrophied landed gentry and similar phenomena
of civilisation will always be adequate myths . . . If ever they
cease to be so, a great deal of past literature will have ceased to
have literary value.' (A.A.P.)
Why is the *Odyssey* still read then, son? (A.P.)
265    the lithe proboscis: our author here imitates the divine Milton,
*Paradise Lost*, IV, 345-7:
               th' unwieldy Elephant
    To make them mirth us'd all his might and wreathd
    His Lith Proboscis.

They greet the Goddess and to partners set,
Small tails like wreathing o'er each massive bum,
And dance the pompous dance of Dunderdom.
The Queen, bewildered by this ponderous show,
270  The sense of their 'enactment' seeks to know.
'Mother,' booms Empson, with a final thud,
'Our convolutions should be clear as mud;
Simplicity, great Queen, is for the birds.
Mark this vast structure built of Complex Words;
Insert a lucid poem; pause, and see
How all dissolves in Ambiguity.'
'All hail, Semantic Father!' answers Brooks.
'For Adumbrations, let her read *my* books,
Explore that intricate, inane Sublime
280  And play cat's-cradle to the end of time.'
'Thank you,' replies the Queen, 'I'd rather not.'
Translates the pair to a remoter spot,
Praises their efforts to enhance her state,
But owns that nine such critics make a Tate.

Now Allen Tate comes on with massive tread:

270    enactment: why do they dance, son? (A.P.)
The modern critics, grandad, like bees before the hive, perform
a sort of dance to indicate where honey flowers are to be found.
This is called 'enacting the meaning'. (A.A.P.)
271    Empson: who is this, son? (A.P.)
The Father of formalist criticism, grandad, author of two famous
works: *Seven Types of Ambiguity* (1930) and *The Structure of
Complex Words* (1951). These are the Old and New Testaments
of this curious religion. (A.A.P.)
277    Brooks: and this? (A.P.)
He wrote the Pauline epistles to the gospels of the Messiah. See
*The Uses of Formal Analysis* (1951): 'The interested reader already
knows the general nature of the critical position adumbrated—or
if he does not, he can find it set forth in writings of mine or of
other critics of like sympathy.' How do you like this? (A.A.P.)
Insolent puppy! (A.P.)
284    Pope, *Epistle to Dr Arbuthnot*:
        All these my modest satire bad translate
        And own that nine such poets made a Tate.

His poems are golden but his prose is lead;
In Labyrinthine coils it crowds and squirms
With knotted syntax and entangled terms,
Strangles each poem, as the serpents once
290   Laocoön and his unhappy sons,
Enfolds and squeezes, crushes and extracts
Small crumbs of meaning and vast files of facts;
The poet crumbles and the reader nods
Yet on and on and on and on he plods.
The tulip's streaks are numbered, all admit,
But is the poem illumined? Not a whit;
For all his purpose is to demonstrate
The sensibilities of Allen Tate.
Alas, his language gives his game away
300   And sets a bound to all he has to say.
The Goddess yawns, the serpent folds untwist
And slough, as Tate and Tedium are dismissed.

But now with heavier beasts the earth is trod:
Blackmur and Northrop Frye with equal plod

295   The tulip's streaks: Dr Johnson, *Rasselas*: 'The business of a poet, said Imlac, is to examine not the individual but the Species . . . he does not number the streaks of the tulip.'

296   illumined: see Allen Tate, 'Tension in Poetry', in *Collected Essays* (1948): 'But convenience of elucidation is not a canon of criticism . . . I do not know what bearing my comment has had, upon the larger effects of poetry . . . I have of necessity confined both commentary and illustration to the slighter effects that seemed to me commensurate with certain immediate qualities of language.'

300   sets a bound: Allen Tate, 'Tension in Poetry': 'For in the long run, whatever the poet's "philosophy", however wide may be the extension of his meaning . . . by his language shall you know him; the quality of his language is the valid limit of what he has to say.' Hoist with his own petard, eh, son? (A.P.)

303   with heavier beasts: our author at this point, son, suddenly recollected the delightful musical parody of Raphael's aria in *The Creation* of Haydn to the words:
        Den Boden drückt der Tiere Last.
In the English version:
        With heavy beasts the earth is trod. (A.P.)

And equal in gravamen, as in groan,
With cumbrous frolics next approach the throne.
Behind them Kenneth Burke and Schorer prate,
Twin masters of the Inarticulate.
They speak no language, mime and reel and sprawl:
310    What does it matter? They 'enact' it all;
For in their doctrine that's the final test
And acrobatic verse is judged the best.
'Tis not enough a poet's lines should flow

308    the Inarticulate: I can scarcely credit this, son: surely two critics of great reputation? (A.P.)
Let me demonstrate, grandad, with typical specimens of the prose of these masters. First, Kenneth Burke, 'Symbolic Action in a Poem by Keats', in *A Grammar of Motive* (1945): 'We might go on to make an infinity of observations about the detail of the stanza; but as regards major deployments we should deem it enough to note that the theme of "pipes and timbrels" is developed by the use of mystic oxymoron, and then surpassed (or given a development-atop-the-development) by the stressing of erotic imagery (that had been ambiguously adumbrated in the references to "maidens loth" and "mad pursuit" of Stanza I). And we could note the quality of *incipience* in this imagery, its state of arrest not at fulfilment, but at the point just prior to fulfilment.' (A.A.P.)
God bless us, son, what would Dryden have said to this ? (A.P.)
He would throw up, grandad. And now for Mark Schorer, *Technique as Discovery* (1948): 'Technique in fiction, all this is a way of saying, we somehow continue to regard as merely a means to organising material which is "given" rather than as the means of exploring and defining the values in an area of experience which, for the first time *then*, are being given.' How is that for incoherence? (A.A.P.)
Crikey, son, now I credit it. (A.P.)
310–16    For a sample of this idea, grandad, I give you a further specimen of grave-digger's prose from Kenneth Burke (ibid.): 'For a poem is an act, the symbolic act of the poet who made it—an act of such a nature that, in surviving as a structure or object, it enables us as readers to re-enact it.'
'Thus the Urn as a viaticum (or rather, with the *poem* as a viaticum and *in the name* of the Urn), having symbolically enacted a kind of act that transcends our mortality, we round out the process by coming to dwell upon the transcendental ground of this act.'
Golly, grandad, do we? (A.A.P.)
Too strenuous for me, son. (A.P.)

With eloquence, with sense and passion glow,
Sing like an angel, speak with grace and tact:
All fails, unless its meaning it 'enact'.

The Queen surveys these antics, turns around
And calls on Frye and Blackmur to expound.
Ere torpid Blackmur rouses to reply
320    Great Frye displays his fearful symmetry;
The multitude draw round to hear him speak;
He preaches a full hour; it seems a week;
And Frye, still preaching in the wilderness,
Regards the hungry multitude's distress;
Still preaching, from his hat he takes a fish
Called William Blake and set it in his dish;
And, preaching still, he lays it on the coals
And, while his magic eloquence unrolls,
A Miracle! the fish becomes a feast
330    Of twenty thousand baskets-full at least.
Alas, the empty multitude is fed
Not meat, but predication, stones for bread.
'Now, having explained my author, I explain
My explanation, brethren, and again
Explain *those* comments, while you break your fast:
To this all literature must come at last!'

The crowd are on their feet! They cheer and sing:
'Reward him, Mighty Mother! Frye for King!'
But, at this music, drowsy Blackmur wakes:

320    his fearful symmetry: what is this, son? (A.P.)
Northrop Frye, *Fearful Symmetry: A study of William Blake* (1947).
Not much symmetry about it, grandad, but fearful enough, and a
very pretty preachment. (A.A.P.)
339–46    Our author here intends a parallel with the incident in the funeral
games of Aeneas, where old Entellus fells a bull with his fist.
Dryden's *Aeneid*, V, 637–41:
    Sternly he spoke; and then confronts the Bull;
    And on his ample forehead aiming full,
    The deadly Stroke descending, pierced the Skull.
    Down drops the Beast; nor needs a second Wound:
    But sprawls in pangs of Death; and spurns the ground. (A.P.)

340　'Still preaching from the pulpit or the jakes!
　　　What? Give the prize to Frye? Make Frye a King?
　　　Promote him to a gibbet: let him swing!
　　　My fist knocks off his sanctimonious hat;
　　　I smite between his horns; take that, and *that*!'
　　　So saying, he strikes; his rival sways; he sprawls;
　　　His breath is spent and like an ox he falls.

　　　The fickle crowd at once begin to cry:
　　　'Crown Blackmur, mighty Queen! A fig for Frye!'
　　　They dance and clap and raise the Victor's Hymn
350　And tear unhappy Northrop limb from limb.
　　　But over all laborious Blackmur's strain,
　　　Still rumbling in the bowels of Hart Crane,
　　　Drowns out their cries and makes the welkin ring:
　　　'Hear me, great Mother, hearken while I sing!
　　　In tortuous syntax, lame and out of hand,

351–62　I thrill to these lines, son, as I did to Mr Pope's lines on this hero's
　　　　sublime ancestor, Sir Richard Blackmore, *Dunciad*, II, 259–68:
　　　　　　But far o'er all, sonorous Blackmore's strain;
　　　　　　Walls, steeples, skies, bray back to him again.
　　　　　　In Tot'nam fields the brethren with amaze
　　　　　　Prick all their ears up and forget to graze . . .
　　　　　　All hail him victor in both gifts of song,
　　　　　　Who sings so loudly, and who sings so long. (A.P.)
355–6　There is a splendid example both of the syntax and the modesty
　　　　of this hero in his 'New Thresholds, New Anatomies: Notes on
　　　　a text of Hart Crane', in *Language as Gesture* (1935): 'Immediately
　　　　following, in the same poem, there is a parenthesis, which I have
　　　　not been able to penetrate with any certainty, though the possi-
　　　　bilities are both fascinating and exciting. The important words in
　　　　it do not possess the excluding power over themselves and their
　　　　relations by which alone the precise, vital element in ambiguity
　　　　is secured. What Crane may have meant privately cannot be in
　　　　question—his words may have represented for him a perfect
　　　　tautology; we are concerned only with how the words act on
　　　　each other—or fail to act—so as to commit an appreciable
　　　　meaning. I quote from the first clause of the parenthesis.
　　　　　　Let sphinxes from the ripe
　　　　　　Borage of death have cleaved my tongue
　　　　　　Once and again . . .' (A.A.P.)
　　　　Surely a lot of palaver to say the *words* have no sense and that *he*
　　　　has no sense of smell. (A.P.)

Explaining what I do not understand;
I cannot tell the Bull's feet from the B's,
Nor see the wood for counting all its trees.
*Lucus a non lucendo* is the fashion,
360    But my impenetrable explication
Earns me the prize (though stultifies the song)
Who say so little and who talk so long.'

The crowd renews its plaudits and its cries
To see great Blackmur crowned and win the Prize;
But Dullness falters, hesitates and hums;
Then springing from her throne, exclaims:

                         'He comes!

He comes, by prophets and by seers foretold,
To usher in my spurious Age of Gold;
Latest of all my sons, my chiefest care,
370    Messiah of Nonsense and great Arthur's Heir!'
Meanwhile her eyes are fixed where, from the east,
A speck, a dot, a blot, a cloud, increased
Moment by moment fascinates each eye
And, speeding towards them, glitters in the sky.
In graceful arcs it spirals, swerves and swoops,
Emitting heavenly Muzak, as it loops;
Light iridescence gleams along its side
—For now 'tis near enough to be descried—
And soon it lands and taxis towards the line,
380    A glistening engine of unknown design.
Swift through the crowd, like cats'-paws o'er a lake,
Conjecture runs with rumour in its wake.
Some say a sputnik and a UFO some,
The Second Coming or the Millennium,
As, from the hatch on top, a curious dome
Of shining perspex and resplendent chrome,
A smiling figure, uniformed in white,
Steps down and blinds them with excess of light.
He stood there—for at least it seemed to be
390    A He—or might, perhaps, it be a She?—

Quite featureless, yet as the crowd look on,
Each seemed by turns to recognize his own;
Then moving like a dancer, proud, serene,
The radiant newcomer salutes the Queen.
'Hail, Mother, late in time behold me come!
To join the Games prescribed at Arthur's Tomb.'
He turns towards the Tomb and kneeling there:
'Great Avatar of Nonsense, hear my prayer!
My time is not yet come, yet here behold
400    Your true Successor by dark stars foretold.
These Esaus spurn, reject their horoscopes
And bless me, Father, Jacob of your hopes!'
The Tomb flies open with a hollow sound,
And coiling up from shades of underground,
A mighty serpent glides, and winks an eye,
And disappears into a bog nearby.

And next the Stranger turns towards the throne:
'The contest, Goddess, let it now go on!
And let me demonstrate before my Queen
410    The sovereign virtues of my blest machine.'
'Alas, dear child, whoever you may be,
Still wrapt in clouds of dim futurity,
The victims whom I raised to demonstrate
Are all used up. Forgive me, you must wait
Till I can summon up, and so I will,
Some modern genius worthy of your skill.'
'Fear not, fond parent,' was the Shade's reply.
'For on mere authors I no more rely;
Now Automation and the Critic's Art
420    Make poets obsolete as horse and cart.

403–6    So at the prayer of Aeneas before the tomb of Anchises. Dryden's
*Aeneid*, Book V:
    Scarce had he finished, when, with speckled pride,
    A serpent from the tomb began to glide;
    His hugy bulk on seven high volumes rolled;
    Blue was his breadth of back, but streaked with scaly gold:
    Thus riding on his curls, he seemed to pass
    A rolling fire along, and singe the grass. (A.P.)

In this superb contraption here, you see
The Self-moved Mover as Machinery;
The Muses are redundant now; and thanks
To automatic brains and memory banks,
Pure Criticism triumphs over all
Without resort to Raw Material.
The Last Age, primitive although it was,
Produced Pure Poetry; eschewed the dross
Of subject, narrative, connective themes;
430   Now ours at last evolves the Dream of Dreams:
Pure Criticism, without thought or fuss;
Pure Theory formed, with nothing to discuss!
This rare device embodies in its guts
No cranks or levers, pistons, cogs or nuts;
A "magic eye" looks inward and controls
Pure Critics musing on their own pure souls.'
A murmur sweeps the mob; the murmur dies
And Dullness rises and bestows the Prize:
'The Works of mighty Arthur, may he live
440   In well-tooled leather, nicely gilt, receive!
Peruse them duly, emulate his fame,
And rule the nations in thy Greater Name!

But now, Young Prophet, we must make an end:
The time has come for Arthur to ascend.
Let all assemble soon to see him rise
And let your plaudits waft him to the skies;
And may this Morning Star his reign forestalls
Stand up and catch his mantle as it falls!'

448   his mantle: so Dryden, *Mac Flecknoe*, 214-17:
        Sinking he left his Drugget robe behind,
        Borne upwards by a subterranean wind.
        The Mantle fell to the young Prophet's part
        With double portion of his Father's Art.  (A.P.)

## *End of Book V*

# BOOK VI

Low on an ebb-tide shore that oozed and stank,
While crowds of envious scribblers lined the bank,
Crowned with fool's parsley, smug with blank content,
Great Arthur sat prepared for his ascent.
His lantern jaws, whose 'uncreating word'
Made darkness visible and sense absurd,
Rehearsed an endless coronation speech,
Unheard amid the cat-calls from the beach.
Rejected suitors for the dunces' crown,
10  If he should rise they hoped to howl him down,
The whole Antipodean regiment
Of bards and critics, gathered to prevent
The deep damnation of his taking off—
But those who came to prey, remained to scoff:
For, lo, attended by a blowsy chain
Of nymphs, sweet daggle-tails, who form her train,
The Mother Goddess suddenly appears
Bearing the sacred ritual asses' ears,
Which none but the true royal line will fit,
20  Those destined on the throne itself to sit.

1    Cf. Milton, *Paradise Lost*, II, 1:
        High on a Throne of Royal State, which far . . .
    and Pope, *Dunciad*, II, 1:
        High on a gorgeous seat, that far outshone
3    'fool's parsley': the victors in the Isthmian and the Nemean
    games wore a parsley crown. (A.P.)
13   Cf. *Macbeth*, Act 1, sc. 7:
        his virtues
       Will plead like angels trumpet-tongued against
       The deep damnation of his taking-off . . . (A.P.)
19-20  So the great son of Uther Pendragon alone could draw the sword
    from the stone in token he should be King. (See Malory's *Morte
    Darthur*.) So too none but Ulysses could bend the mighty bow
    in token he *was* the King. (A.P.)

She claps them on his skull: They stick! They grow!
Frame the *pons asinorum* of his brow,
And instant, from his throat burst such a bray
As struck his rivals speechless with dismay.
A second, third deep bombinating yell—
Down like rejected manuscripts they fell;
Flat as their works, in hecatombs they lie,
One seething, pullulating printer's pie!

And now the goddess his ascent prepares;
30    But first she calls to sacrifice and prayers.
An altar of the critic's works she builds
Which Merdamant with bilge-and-bitters gilds;
Sweet Cloacina lights the sullen flame,
While Arthur calls his ancestors by name.
Then on the pyre the works of Pope he cast—

There was a sudden, bright, ethereal blast;
A pure, intense, reverberating light
One instant gave the purblind creatures sight:
One instant all the deep of heaven lay bare,
40    They saw and understood the vision there;
The mystic harmony, the primal law
And Art with Nature joined in dance they saw;
They felt the rage of genius in them mount,
And the high scorn that guards the sacred fount.

23    He makes me slay the suitors *before* I get home, grandad! (A.A.P.)
      Natural enough to you to get things back to front, son. (A.P.)
32–3  Merdamant . . . Cloacina: these two nymphs whose names
      sufficiently indicate the streams over which they preside, our
      author hath borrowed from Mr Pope, *Dunciad*, II, 93:
          In office here fair Cloacina stands,
          And ministers to Jove with purest hands.
          First he relates how sinking to the chin,
          Smit with his mein the Mud-nymphs suck'd him in,
          How Young Lutetia, softer than the down
          Nigrina black and Merdamante brown . . .
                                    (ibid., 331) (A.P.)

One instant—it was over in a flash:
Once more opinionated, oafish, brash,
They chased the fading vision from the brain
And blundered back into themselves again.
At last with awful voice the Goddess cries:
50 'It is the hour! Behold your monarch rise!
(Look lively, girls, and help him off his bum!)
And all ye powers of darkness, watch him come!'

As when Aunt Tabitha at eighty-eight,
Defying ground and gravity and Fate,
Scorns the embraces of the devious train,
And, greatly daring, goes by aeroplane;
Too late, too late with sinking heart she sees
Earth fall away with all its roofs and trees;
Instead of soaring bird-like o'er the town,
60 She feels the ground drop off, the sky swoop down,
And in her heart of hearts, suspects a plot,
By Nature on Mechanic Art begot:
All the resources of the engineer,
The wealth of some great transport profiteer,
Turned to one end, designed with fiendish skill
To hoodwink, elevate, trepan and kill
By inches in their devilish machine
One scared old lady in black bombazine—
So Dullness all her latent power displays
70 Her favourite from obscurity to raise.
Nausea, her handmaid, there with Nonsense vies
To elevate one pedant to the skies.
In vain his tutelary muses strain,
Heave, haul and flap their moulting wings in vain:
The Goddess sees him cold and flat and dense—
She calls the new Tenth Muse of Impudence:

53-72 A delightful example of the Homeric simile, son! (A.P.)
Pish! (A.A.P.)

'Descend, Publicity, ingenious Frump!
Swiftly inflate him with thy Patent Pump!'
She comes; she puffs; he swells—Behold him rise
80    Like a blown bull-frog croaking to the skies!
Aloft he rose, majestic, wobbling, slow,
While one nymph hauled and one pushed up below.
Wild shrieks of 'Arthur!' waft him from the ground;
And 'Arthur!' swamps and fens and bogs resound.

But earthly sounds grow fainter in his ear;
The ancient towers of Dullness soon appear.
Now one more struggle! Veering towards the moon,
He drifts and bobs like an escaped balloon.
While lovely Nonsense, fat and all aglow,
90    Giggles and heaves the mighty bulk below,
Fair Nausea, head down and heels in air,
Pulls, puffs, and sweeps him with her pendant hair,
Struggles to steer and strives amain to lift,
While round her ears descends her artless shift,
And, upside-down her ample form displays
One vast, blown blush to everybody's gaze.

So they arrive, are hailed, hauled in and stand
At last rejoicing on the promised land.
And now towards the venerable pile,
100   Built in the railway-station-gothic style,
The hero ambles and turns in the gate
Above the lintel, in decrepit state,
The ancient owl of Dullness preened its wing
And was the first to know and greet her King.

103ff.   So Homer (Pope's *Odyssey*, Book XVII):
       Thus near the gates, conferring as they drew,
       Argus, the dog, his ancient master knew
       And where on heaps the rich manure was spread
       Obscene with reptiles took his sordid bed,
       He knew his lord; he knew and strove to meet
       In vain he strove to crawl and kiss his feet. (A.P.)

Moulting and moping on its perch, the bird
Let fall, upon his head one funeral merd,
And, with one squawk, fell fluttering beneath
His foot, and turned its eyelids up in death.

Now through the portal, issuing at a run,
110    The grandsire welcomes the prodigious son:
'My long-lost heir, my dab-chick, my absurd
Sweet mopoke, my Australian thunderbird—'
The good old sire here stopped and wept for joy—
'How nice to see you, welcome home my boy!
My Duck-billed Paradox, at last we meet!
Come to my arms!
              And thou, majestic seat
That groaned beneath so many royal Kings,
Receive thy new Possessor! One who brings
A mind not to be swayed by this or that—
120    Having, indeed, no mind beneath his hat!'

'Darkling I listen!' then replied the son,
'With signal portents has my reign begun:
Henceforth I will . . . Henceforth . . . Tut! I can not
Remember *what* henceforth I would have what!'

107    merd: an unusual word. See T. S. Eliot's euphonious line:
        Rocks, moss, stone-crop, iron, merd. ('Gerontion') See also his:
        'Merd: Or In the Cathedral.' (A.A.P.)
112    thunderbird: the Australian shrike or thick-head, *Pachycephala gutturalis.*
113    Cf. Dryden, *Mac Flecknoe:*
        Here stopped the good old sire, and wept for joy.
115    the Platypus: *Ornithorynchus paradoxus,* I should have said—I had
        specially learned these Antipodean terms of endearment to please
        him. (A.P.)
116ff.    Cf. *Paradise Lost,* Book I:
        and thou profoundest Hell
        Receive thy new Possessor: One who brings
        A mind not to be chang'd by Place or Time.    (A.P.)
121    Darkling: 'to darkle' is the opposite of 'to sparkle'—here a quo-
        tation from my grandson's favourite poem—actually quoted in
        the broadcast which was the original seed of his fame. (A.P.)

'Oh Death!' rejoined the sire, with joyful squeaks.
'O Eloquence! In oracles he speaks!
The brain is clouded: Grieve not, noble Heart!
It is the air affects the thinking part.
With me indeed, indeed it was the same
130    When first to these high altitudes I came:
On earth I showed just moderately dense
But here I have not spoke one word of sense.

But come, I long to see thee on thy throne,
I, that got Kings though I myself was none!
Come, let these eyes thy consummation see
And my last pastoral be writ for thee,
To tell, while flocks of dunces round thee stand,
"How well the crook beseems thy lilly hand." '

He said; and led him to the castle hall.
140    There sat the ghostly dunces, drowsing all,
Scribbled or argued, ranted, mused or taught—
Blank were the pages still, the words meant nought,
And blank the faces turned to greet their King
And blank their silence at his home-coming.
But he, through all their ranks unmoved strides on,
Mounts the worn steps and stands before the Throne,
One long, triumphant moment: then he turns
And faces them; with conscious pride he burns;
He takes and tries the royal crown: It fits!
150    He bends his knees; his hams; he bumps; he SITS!

---

134    This is the prophetic line referred to before, adapted by our
author from the divine Shakespeare. (A.P.)
Stolen, you mean. (A.A.P.)
138    Here, here at last our author quotes a line from one of my own
pastorals—one of the finest samples of the Namby-Pamby style
(*First Pastoral*: Ambrose Philips):
How would the crook beseem thy lilly-hand!
How would my younglings round thee gazing stand!
Ah, witless younglings! gaze not on her eye:
Thence all thy sorrow; thence the death I dy.

He sat, and waited with expectant ears
To hear their loyal, royal unmeaning cheers—
O, horror!  Through the host from door to door
Rank after rank slides gently to the floor;
Rank upon rank they lie like folded sheep,
Mumbling immortal nonsense in their sleep.
And next the King himself begins to nod,
The last, great conquest of the drowsy god;
Thy hand, great Anarch, softly draws the blind
160   And one vast snore seals the eclipse of mind.


151–6   So Satan (*Paradise Lost*, X, 504–9):
             So having said, awhile he stood, expecting
             Thir universal shout and high applause
             To fill his eare when contrary he hears
             On all sides, from innumerable tongues
             A dismal universal hiss . . .


*Finis*